Life as a Junior Barrister

This essential volume for all aspiring barristers offers guidance, insights and advice from new barristers from a diverse range of backgrounds and practice areas, shedding light on what life is really like for barristers at the independent Bar.

Each chapter is candid and honest about the reality of the Bar and how it measures against student expectations. There is only one Bar, but working in different practice areas brings different challenges. This book brings together new practitioners from across the disciplines, from crime to commercial, from family to employment law, and more, as they each discuss their workloads, the sorts of cases and tasks that they typically face and highlight the skills which need to be developed in the first couple of years. Practical tips around time-management and finance feature, as well as advice around key social and cultural issues. The concluding chapter by Jaime Hamilton QC discusses the transformations that the Bar has undergone and continues to go through.

Accessible and engaging, this invaluable resource is the perfect guide for anyone interested in exploring a career at the Bar. It will be an ideal companion to students of law at any level.

Nigel Booth is the Programme and Student Experience Lead for the Bar Practice Course at the University of Law's Manchester and Liverpool campuses. He was called to the Bar by Gray's Inn in 1994 and has worked as a barrister for 25 years.

Life as a Junior Barrister

In the Words of the Independent Bar

Edited by
Nigel Booth

Routledge
Taylor & Francis Group
LONDON AND NEW YORK

Cover image: ©istock/ bpperry

First published 2023
by Routledge
4 Park Square, Milton Park, Abingdon, Oxon OX14 4RN

and by Routledge
605 Third Avenue, New York, NY 10158

Routledge is an imprint of the Taylor & Francis Group, an informa business

British Library Cataloguing-in-Publication Data
A catalogue record for this book is available from the British Library

Library of Congress Cataloging-in-Publication Data
A catalog record has been requested for this book

ISBN: 978-0-367-62959-5 (hbk)
ISBN: 978-0-367-56649-4 (pbk)
ISBN: 978-1-003-11159-7 (ebk)

DOI: 10.4324/9781003111597

Typeset in Sabon
by Deanta Global Publishing Services, Chennai, India

Contents

Foreword — *vii*
His Honour Judge Maurice Greene, Manchester Crown Court, Minshull Street, Manchester

Introduction — 1
Nigel Booth, Programme Lead for the Bar Practice Course, University of Law

1 **Family Law** — 8
An Interview with Malvika Jaganmohan, St Ives Chambers

2 **Commercial Chancery** — 23
An Interview with Ted Loveday, Maitland Chambers

3 **Civil, Personal Injury, Clinical Negligence** — 39
An Interview with Rebecca Titus-Cobb, St John's Buildings Chambers

4 **Property, Planning, Public Law** — 52
An Interview with Joel Semakula, Landmark Chambers

5 **Inquests, Public Law** — 65
An Interview with Ciara Bartlam, Garden Court North Chambers

6 **Crime, Social Mobility** — 80
An Interview with Danielle Manson, Garden Court Chambers

7 **Employment, Planning, Crime** — 88
An Interview with Angelica Rokad, 6 Pump Court Chambers

8 **Commercial Law** **104**
An Interview with Sophia Dzwig, 3 Verulam Buildings

9 **Crime** **117**
An Interview with Tony Williams, Central Chambers, Manchester

10 **Looking Back and Going Forwards: Reflections of a Modern Silk** **138**
Jaime Hamilton QC, 9 St John Street Chambers, Manchester

Index *145*

Foreword

As a circuit judge sitting in Manchester, I have the opportunity of having many new members of the Bar appear before me on a daily basis. However, I do not get the opportunity to speak to them about their day-to-day experiences of practice, which is likely to be very different than my own back in the early 1980s. When I was a new barrister, I did not specialise in any particular field and, like many, I took any work that was offered to me. Over the last 20 years or so there has been a move towards specialisation at an earlier stage than before. It seems that people are often required to choose their path when they apply for pupillage, even though they may not be entirely sure themselves that they've chosen the correct path. This is one reason why I believe this book provides such invaluable information for those considering a career at the Bar. The interviewees specialise in many different areas of law and give a true picture of what life is like during the early years of practice at the Bar.

When I left the Inns of Court School of Law to enter the world of pupillage in 1982, I knew how to draft particulars of claim, conduct a bail application, a plea in mitigation and write an Advice, but I had very little idea about the realities of life during the early years of practice at the Bar. What is life really like in Chambers? What sort of clients would I have? How much work could I expect? How much could I really hope to earn? How do I look after my own wellbeing? How do I get work? There have always been legal textbooks, books on advocacy and drafting, but rarely is there a book that contains such practical information. This is that book.

I have known Nigel Booth for more than 20 years from when he was a young prosecutor to when he became a colleague in Chambers and latterly as an advocate appearing in front of me. Meticulous in everything he does, it does not surprise me that he should have conceived the idea to create and edit such a book as this. Nigel has always been interested in research going beyond that which is normally undertaken at the Bar, having advised on research into jury decision-making and written books to assist litigants in person. As one can see from this volume, Nigel has a particular interest in assisting those who may be considering becoming a barrister as well as those who have already embarked on their careers. He has used his considerable experience of practice at the Bar to tease out a considerable amount of valuable information from his interviewees, who have been candid about their experiences.

This book provides a unique insight into the real-life experiences of barristers during their early years of practice. Everyone from the A-level student contemplating a career at the Bar to the pupillage applicant anxiously considering their choices as the gateway opens should read this book to understand what they may face in those first years in the profession. It should be part of every budding barrister's library, as it is likely to become as important as any legal textbook.

His Honour Judge Maurice Greene
Manchester Crown Court
Minshull Street, Manchester
January 2022

Introduction

In March 2020 I received an urgent telephone call from a judge at one of the Crown Courts that I had been attending regularly as a barrister for 20 years. One of my prosecution cases was listed before him later that day for me to offer no evidence. The police, CPS and I had decided that there was no longer a realistic prospect of conviction. It was a sound decision, and I was not expecting any problems. 'Do not come to court!' the judge ordered me. 'It is not safe!' This was my first real introduction to the devastation that Covid-19 would wreak on a criminal justice system that was already weak at the knees. It had been brought close to death by a decade of a thousand cuts, and Covid was just starting to twist the knife.

But this is not a book about Covid-19. Nor is it about just the criminal bar. The idea for it first came to me in early 2018 during a conversation with the psychologist Dr Dominic Willmott with whom I had been collaborating in a major jury research project into rape myths. In a Huddersfield coffee shop, we came to be discussing how I had started out in the law, and out of the blue I asked myself what was it like starting out at the Bar today? I knew what it had been like to start out at the Bar in criminal law 25 years previously, but that was hardly a guide for the 2020s! Equally, I had absolutely no idea what it is like for a new barrister starting out in Chambers in employment, or commercial, or family, or public, or any one of the other many fields of law that exist beyond a Bar training course. What sorts of cases do you do as a new practitioner? Who are your clients typically? What tasks come your way; in a real sense, what do you actually *do*? What are the greatest challenges? How much work is there? What might new barristers expect to earn across all the different practice areas? And I thought to myself, wouldn't it be a good idea to interview new barristers in different fields of law, and then gather the interviews in one book. It would be an instant guide for any student considering a career at the Bar.

This is that book.

I did not know when I started out on the project for this book that just six months later I would be teaching trainee barristers on the Bar Practice

DOI: 10.4324/9781003111597-1

Course (BPC) at the University of Law's Manchester campus, that we would soon be running those BPC classes at the University of Liverpool's School of Law and Social Justice, and that I would become the Programme Lead for both cities. Strange how life works out. The same month when Covid hit the courts, I got together with Routledge Publishing and set about interviewing junior barristers within their first two or three years of practice at the independent Bar so that I could gather their experiences of practice. I am careful to say 'the independent Bar' so that you understand we are dealing with barristers who work out of one or more of the hundreds of barristers' Chambers across England and Wales. This book is for you if you are considering a career at the independent Bar.

The route that students take to the independent Bar has not changed very much over the years, although there is change visible on the horizon as new routes are proposed for students to become barristers. The best source of information about such changes will always be the website of the Bar Council of England and Wales at www.barcouncil.org.uk. Typically, you may go to Bar School and after graduation you will undertake 12 months' training in Chambers called a pupillage, which is subject to a minimum income scheme. In your second six months you will have rights of audience and can take cases of your own in court, and then after pupillage you would then apply for a tenancy in your Chambers. In my day, a Chambers might have had any number of pupils, only a couple of whom would ultimately be taken on as tenants, but these days Chambers tend to take on pupils for whom they hold out the greatest tenancy hope.

Let us dispel some myths first. You don't have to go to Bar School; there are plenty of barristers who qualified first as solicitors and later transferred across to Chambers. You don't have to do pupillage in Chambers; the Crown Prosecution Service and Government Legal Service are two examples of organisations that offer pupillage, and now many solicitors' firms are able to offer pupillages, too. (I did my pupillage with the Crown Prosecution Service back in 1994 before moving a few years later to the independent Bar.) The employed Bar is a large and varied group. Perhaps the biggest myth of all is that to get to Bar School you must first have completed a law degree. You don't! If you study something else for your degree, you just need an extra year's qualifying study on a course called the GDL, or Graduate Diploma in Law, though there are others. Some of my interviewees, among them Sophia Dzwig and Ciara Bartlam, came to the Bar this way. It is not an uncommon route, and it is certainly not perceived as second class.

I was interested to learn from the interviews that I conducted for this book that in its content, the Bar course had not changed very much since

I studied it back in 1993. The Bar training courses offered to trainee barristers by my university and by other providers must continue to teach the knowledge areas of criminal and civil litigation and the various Bar skills deemed necessary by the regulator, the Bar Standards Board (BSB), although recently the BSB has permitted the providers a greater degree of latitude in how they structure their courses. Has anything surprised me from my interviews conducted more than 25 years after I studied for the Bar? Plenty. It has been interesting to speak to new barristers practising in areas of law outside the narrow confines of criminal and civil litigation taught on the Bar course and hear them reflect on the extent to which they use in practice their learning from the Bar course. Often, they don't use their knowledge of criminal and civil litigation at all; their practice areas have their own rules and regulations. For many, therefore, the usefulness of the knowledge part of the training lies in developing a close familiarity with rules-based thinking. In non-criminal practice areas, drafting skills continue to be highly relevant, typically when it comes to the drafting of pleadings such as particulars of claim. Opinion-writing as a skill seems to be evolving in practice as barristers deal increasingly with gradual requests for advice by e-mail. Advocacy has always been a staple ingredient of the course, and it continues to be a skill deployed across many practice areas; yet it is easy to overlook that there are many, many barristers who hardly ever engage in advocacy. Many advocates practise in areas of law where wigs and gowns are not used, for instance in the coroners' courts and in family courts. Of all the skills taught on the course, though, there is one that is a mainstay of every case up and down the country for every practising barrister: the ability to conduct an effective conference. This is the universal skill. Mastering this skill at an early stage helps students organise the taking of instructions and the giving of advice in a constructive way so that the conference is not a mere conversation, and all the barristers I spoke to for this book appreciated that.

One thing that surprised me is that new barristers today seem to specialise less narrowly than used to be the case. In their pupillage offerings, Chambers have always tried to offer a range of experience. The general common law pupillage has perhaps been the best example of that because pupils get a basic grounding in crime and civil cases. But what I mean when I say I have been surprised is that now even into tenancy, new barristers tend to maintain a wide scope of practice. This fits with the modern multi-disciplinary approach of many Chambers, allowing their barristers to take on a diverse, in the sense of varied, caseload.

Several times over, my interviewees were clear about what any Bar course *cannot* teach: how to balance and prioritise the many tasks that a growing case load continually generates. This is a real skill that cannot be learned other than in the job, although in a sense the Bar course does inadvertently 'help' students with this on account of the immense volume of work that it generates each week. The best students are those who have developed effective time management and prioritisation skills. Whilst there is much technique to be learned in the way of interpersonal and written skills, some of which are live and involve actors who play the role of the client or the witness, there is still a significant amount of reading for the civil and criminal litigation assessments, and it must all be understood at a level that is both fundamental and detailed.

I found among my interviewees a real awareness of the need to maintain wellbeing, so often a word that has been used too readily without being properly thought through. The new barristers of today appreciate more than ever the need to maintain a healthy balance between work and home life. This doesn't only mean having meaningful pastimes away from work, though that is in itself of very great importance. It also means being able to have an open dialogue with the clerks in Chambers so that you take on a level of work that fits your capacity and so that you can take 'paper days' out of court in order to catch up on your prep work. There is little point relentlessly taking on court work if the back of your mind is constantly worrying about the reading and preparation you need to do on your other cases. You need know that your clerks are understanding of this and view it positively. The barristers I interviewed had good experiences of their Chambers' support for their wellbeing and career progression, which after all go hand in hand.

There has been much introspection over recent years as the Bar Council, and the profession has considered the lack of progress when it comes to race and sex. Nowhere have the racial disparities been set out more clearly than by a Bar Council Race Working Group, co-chaired by Barbara Mills QC and Simon Regis. In November 2021, the Working Group published a thorough report titled 'Race at the Bar: A Snapshot'. A glance at just the executive summary reveals some breath-taking statistics and compels further reading. Bar School graduates from ethnic minority backgrounds are less likely to obtain pupillage than their contemporaries who are from white backgrounds. In respect of practising barristers, the report states:

> Women earn on average less than men; Black men earn less than White men; and Black and Asian women earn less than Black and Asian men, and Black women earn the least.

When it comes to QC and judicial appointments, the report is just as plain that the legal profession has a long road to travel to equality.

One interviewee expresses her thoughts like this:

> I don't know if I would go so far as to say that I have experienced discrimination necessarily, but I am very aware of the fact that in order to be an effective advocate as a female you have to work twice as hard as your male contemporaries and that hasn't changed at the Bar.

and

> I don't want white, straight male barristers to fail. I don't want their power; I just want my own power.

Another interviewee told me:

> The Bar is not diverse. It's not a meritocracy either. It's a very old institution with very old, ingrained prejudices that is going to take a very long time to dislodge. I had a work experience student who said to me that she hadn't seen many other people who looked like me on the profiles of Chambers' websites – that had been my experience as well.

The interviews in this book were conducted before the Working Group report was published. The barristers who are interviewed speak for themselves, as you will read, though it seems to me that there is a plainly held view that the Bar needs to do more to make sure that it is properly representative of the society that it serves, and there is a real drive to make the profession as open as it can be to new entrants, wherever they come from. That commitment among the newest entrants provides the strongest hope that the Bar is changing. I detect a real seriousness at the Bar of today to bring about that change. The Working Group report therefore comes at both a critical and an opportune time. There are nearly two dozen recommendations aimed at Chambers, specialist Bar associations and other stakeholders for specific action to address access, retention, progression and Bar culture.

The costs of further education can be problematic, if not prohibitive, for many hopeful entrants to the profession. Danielle Manson, who has a most powerful story behind her route to the Bar, sees social mobility as being a serious challenge for today's Bar, and she is right. Danielle puts it like this:

> The way that social mobility can be advanced in the profession is through doing things like this and talking about my journey

> so that hopefully other people read it and are inspired, or at least assured that not everyone is handed everything on a silver platter. With a little bit of hard work and with the support of some incredible organisations you can overcome that hurdle. Just encouraging people not to self- eliminate is important.

My interviewees discussed with me the initiatives that they are engaging with, sometimes with their Chambers and sometimes more widely, to reach out and show our young people from all economic backgrounds that there is a career at the Bar. There is funding available, too. The university that I work for offers scholarships, as do the four Inns of Court. There are other initiatives. Individual Chambers, even some individual barristers, run their own work experience opportunities, increasingly with expenses paid. My own Chambers at 9 St John Street in Manchester, for example, and in particular our Deputy Head of Chambers Jaime Hamilton QC, set out to make a real difference by spending time, effort and money to bring the Bar to as many people from as many backgrounds as possible. Search out opportunities like this on the internet; they are increasingly there to be found.

Sadly, I cannot tell you that there are no challenges and no obstacles in the path of students who would like to practise at the independent Bar. You probably didn't expect otherwise, anyway. Getting good results in examinations is just the start of the process and in itself guarantees nothing. It is a long and uncertain road, and the fact that it has always been like that is only a little comfort. Being at the Bar is a very rewarding career for those of us who are fortunate to make it.

To the fabulous and impressive junior barristers who agreed to be interviewed for this book, my very great thanks; I am grateful to all of you for taking the time to discuss your careers and thereby helping the barristers of tomorrow make sound decisions about their studies today. I would ask the reader of this book to remain aware that with every passing day, these barristers' careers will develop and change. The interviews reflect the barristers' careers at a point in time a couple of years or so after pupillage, the aim being to show what those early years are like across the various fields of practice.

To my very good friend and Deputy Head of Chambers, Jaime Hamilton QC, a well-known and longstanding barrister of the Northern Circuit, I thank you for contributing your words of experience to this book. Jaime does a tremendous amount to help students gain a foothold, I have already discussed that above. I also would like to thank Julie Burns. Julie and I met when we worked together at a previous Chambers. Julie is an experienced legal secretary with a keen eye for detail, and I could not have asked for anyone better to transcribe the interviews.

The legal work out there at the Bar is wide and varied, and if this book introduces you to what life is like as a junior barrister in different areas of practice then it will have achieved its purpose.

Nigel Booth
Programme and Student Experience Lead for the Bar Practice Course
University of Law, Manchester and Liverpool Campuses
Spring 2022

1 Family Law

An Interview with Malvika Jaganmohan, St Ives Chambers

NB: *Welcome to Malvika Jaganmohan from St Ives Chambers in Birmingham. I know that you are a family practitioner, Malvika. When did you begin tenancy?*

MJ: I became a tenant at St Ives Chambers in Birmingham in November 2019. I did pupillage at a different set of Chambers in London and that started in October 2018, but I had a very serious mental health crisis during my pupillage year after my second six started, so my pupillage was extended by a month because I took a month out. I started tenancy shortly after that at St Ives.

NB: *Did you always want to do what you are doing now?*

MJ: I am definitely not one of those people who came out of the womb wanting to be a family barrister, that's for sure. I did a law degree because I thought it would be an interesting degree to do, not necessarily because I wanted to be a lawyer at the end of it. I did consider becoming a solicitor in a big city firm because they were marketing left, right and centre on campus. Of course, it seemed very exciting, glamorous and inviting. After a few vacation schemes, very well-paid vacation schemes I should say, I decided it clearly wasn't for me. So, I did mini-pupillages at a lot of Chambers in lots of different areas of law, and family law was what I really took to. I had already found it academically interesting. I had a fantastic tutor called Helen Reece, and aside from it just being this socially and politically fascinating area of law, it's such a privilege to have access to the most intimate aspects of clients' private lives. I loved the idea of being a barrister, but I was pretty scared about applying for pupillage because I knew the statistics were grim in terms of obtaining a pupillage. I enjoyed public speaking and I thought the Bar would be a good fit. I applied for a scholarship at my Inn and was

DOI: 10.4324/9781003111597-2

awarded a major scholarship which made the decision for me and gave me the confidence to do the Bar course and apply for pupillage because that financial risk was mitigated.

I applied for pupillage while I was at Bar School and was lucky enough to get it. There is a huge dose of luck involved in getting pupillage as well as hard work and aptitude, but I very much took my journey to the Bar year-by-year. I tried not to get my hopes up too much and I wasn't one of those people who thought, if I can't be a barrister, I can't do anything else. I just wanted to do something meaningful, whether that was the Bar or something else. I'm very happy I'm a family barrister but when I was younger it wasn't my dream job or anything like that.

NB: *It is interesting to compare the routes people take. The reason why I chose to study law at university was (and I'm a little ashamed to say this really) because I couldn't think of anything else to do that would interest me. That's dreadful! I should have been driven and committed but I wasn't, I was just interested. Like you, I did my law degree in London. I did a summer placement at a city solicitors' firm after my second year, and that convinced me more than anything that I wanted to do crime.*

MJ: I do wonder if I'd have had a different view on becoming a barrister versus a solicitor if I had shadowed some family solicitors. I was doing all this work experience in corporate and real estate. Having said that, now that I'm in practice I do think that I'm better suited to the Bar than to being a solicitor because I don't think I have the wherewithal to have that level of client contact. It's an exhausting job because of the nature of the work we do. Solicitors have that on-going, constant contact with the client whereas I have a professional barrier, which is the solicitor, and they tend to do the paperwork and the compliance with directions.

NB: *Can I ask what sort of work your practice takes in? I think family practitioners tend to go into finance work or children work – is that right?*

MJ: I think that's a fair observation. I think some Chambers tend to do more children work, some Chambers tend to do more finance work, but some Chambers do a mix. When I was looking for a Chambers to join for tenancy, I really wanted a Chambers that would give me the opportunity to do everything, just so I would know what it was like, and then maybe further down in my practice, five or ten years from now, I could specialise more if that's what I feel I need to do. That's part of the reason why I joined St Ives as there is a lot of high quality, financial remedies work in Birmingham, and I had almost exclusively been exposed to children work during pupillage. We did a pupil exchange so a pupil at a matrimonial finance set came to my Chambers and then I went to that set and shadowed the practitioners there for a week.

Part of the reason why I joined St Ives was so that I could do all areas of family law. I deal with applications under Part IV of the Family Law Act 1996 (for example, non-molestation orders or occupation orders where domestic abuse is alleged); I do private law children which is disputes between parents, usually about where a child should live and how much contact they should have with the other parent; I do care proceedings, where the state's involved to protect children; and I do financial remedies after separation.

NB: *I wonder if you could give me some examples of the types of cases that you are instructed in right now?*

MJ: In the next couple of months, I have a few final hearings coming up that are multi-day trials in public law proceedings. In some I'm acting for the local authority and in others I'm on the parents' side. I have final hearings coming up in private law matters as well. A few are for long-standing clients that I have represented over many, many months so it will be good to see those coming to a conclusion. Directions hearings are a pretty common feature of my diary where the court is just deciding how to proceed, taking stock, deciding what evidence do we need to line up to get us to a final hearing, but substantive decisions aren't necessarily made. I have a few fact-finding hearings coming up which is where serious allegations have been made, usually of domestic abuse or non-accidental injury to a child, and the court has to determine whether or not they are true before it can move on to make decisions about the children.

NB: *I know a bit about fact-finding hearings because often they can give rise to parallel criminal proceedings.*

MJ: Yes. There is an interesting interplay between the family and the criminal jurisdictions. We obviously use a different standard of proof in family law, on the balance of probabilities, which is a lower standard of proof because of course we are dealing with risk to children. Family practitioners seem to be far more risk-averse and far more cautious in how we approach our cases.

NB: *Criminal cases tend to focus on the wrongdoing, don't they, and the punishing of a particular incident, but in the Family Court you are looking to the on-going safety of people, and that makes it more pressing, I think?*

MJ: Yes. The Family Court isn't about attributing blame or punishing anyone. The goal is different than in the Criminal Court. The reason we have fact-finding hearings in domestic abuse matters is to keep victims of abuse safe. The reason we have fact-finding hearings in children matters is not to mud sling or to find out who is the bad guy, it's with a view to reaching a decision which is safe and productive for the child and which has their best interests in mind and which can hopefully allow this family to move forward in a way that they can live with. There's a lot of long-term thinking in family cases.

On the interplay of the two jurisdictions, in season 1, episode 3 of my podcast *Professionally Embarrassing* we cover the really interesting case of *Re: H-N* which is a landmark appeal concerning the approach taken by the Family Court to allegations of domestic abuse in private law children cases, and there's a section in the judgment about how criminal law concepts should be used in the Family Court. As a family lawyer, I could name various examples of the Family Court importing the approach taken in the Criminal Court. For instance, family law judges routinely give themselves a Lucas direction, about the approach to be taken to lies; that is drawn from the criminal case of *R v Lucas*. However, *Re: H-N* reminds us we should avoid becoming too inappropriately drawn into criminal law concepts in the Family Court. Judges should look at parties' behaviour holistically rather than getting too hung up on the detail of the elements of specific criminal offences when determining whether or not something has or has not happened. The example the Court of Appeal in *Re: H-N* gives is that the Family Court may find that an injury was caused but it doesn't need to get bogged down in whether that would amount to actual bodily harm or grievous bodily harm in a criminal context. It's a really interesting case. I would recommend reading it.

NB: *Can we turn to the sort of tasks that you do in your job that might perhaps be recognisable to students at Bar School?*

MJ: I'm in court a lot. In a typical week, I will be in court at least three or four times, sometimes five, and maybe more than five if I'm doing multiple hearings in a day. Being in court and being an advocate is a big part of my job. On a typical case I would receive the papers, read them, draft a position statement on the basis of the instructions that I have. The papers can come in very last minute; they can come in the night before or the morning of or a few hours before the hearing, and you just have to get to grips with it as best as you can.

NB: *What's a position statement?*

MJ: A position statement is there to assist the court with what the issues are and what your client's position is in respect of the issues. You might also cover any relevant law. There's an expectation, particularly in care matters, that there will be a position statement. I have certainly been told off for not having prepared a position statement even though on legal aid matters you aren't paid for prep. I am in the habit of drafting a position statement even when it's not strictly needed because I find it's quite a useful way to marshal what the issues are and what my client's view is on each of them. Then I usually speak to the client and the other side in the hour before the hearing is listed for pre-hearing discussions, see what the issues are and whether they can be narrowed. That usually involves trying to keep my client on point and on topic because I will only have half an hour to speak to them. Of course, I will advise my client as appropriate on the issues that might arise in the hearing.

At the moment, most of my hearings are taking place remotely, although the number of in-person hearings are starting to pick up again now. What happens in the hearing very much depends on what type of hearing it is; sometimes it can be five minutes, sometimes you go in thinking it will be five minutes and it lasts the whole day, and it may be necessary to call witnesses and to cross-examine them or it's just a matter where you address the judge in submissions, and you don't have to call any witnesses. If it's a final hearing, after evidence is given, the court will require you to make either oral submissions or give written submissions summarising the issues in the case, your client's position and the evidence. After the hearing, the order has to be drafted, agreed with the other parties and then I need to update my solicitor on what happened.

NB: *You actually get involved in drafting the court's order arising out of the hearing?*

MJ: Yes. It's expected that the representative for the applicant drafts the order and circulates it to everyone else for agreement and if the applicant is not represented, then it's the other represented party who has to draft it and get it agreed between everyone, and then we send in an agreed order for the judge to approve. It can be a bit of a nightmare getting an order approved especially if you are against a litigant in person. With a solicitor or another barrister, you feel more comfortable negotiating with them about the contents of an order, but with a litigant in person, you need to be more cautious because you don't want to put undue pressure on them or be perceived to be pulling the wool over their eyes.

NB: *You're talking about reducing into writing the order that the judge gave orally during the hearing?*

MJ: Yes. What generally happens in care matters is that the local authority advocate will prepare a draft order when they are sending in the case summary, and there will be discussions before the hearing when the advocates will talk about the draft order and talk about things that need to go in it, and things that don't, and hopefully an agreed order can be sent to the court ahead of the hearing. It can be tweaked afterwards.

NB: *What sorts of people or organisations have largely been your clients?*

MJ: I've increasingly been doing a lot of work for the local authority, but when I'm not for a local authority, the bulk of my clients are distressed individuals in the middle of a family dispute or clients at risk of having children removed from their care. I often represent some of the most vulnerable members of our society, people with learning difficulties, victims of domestic abuse. I have represented children. It's a pretty mixed bag.

NB: *Can I just ask you about your case load and what that's been like compared with your second six?*

MJ: I think I had a pretty relaxed second six. I remember being so frustrated in my first week because I was hyped to get on my feet and I didn't get a case until the Friday! At the time, I was very stressed and I thought of every case as being of Supreme Court level importance which of course, it wasn't. Tenancy was a bit of a baptism of fire because I went from relatively straightforward matters in pupillage to lengthy final hearings, fact-finds, contested trials.

Anecdotally, the quality of my work improved massively when I left London (though, of course, I was a tenant in Birmingham as opposed to a pupil in London). I don't know if that's because there is so much more competition in London for that junior-level work. Now that I've left London, I find myself doing work at a level that I don't think I would have come anywhere near had I stayed in London. Many of my peers in London don't seem to be doing the sort of work I am.

NB: *That's interesting because sometimes people can think they've got to practise in London because that's where all the good work is.*

MJ: That's very much what I thought. I had always envisaged my practice being in London and being a high-flying London lawyer, but I had these health difficulties during my pupillage year, and I had a bit of a re-assessment and I found that I wasn't very happy in London and I wanted to be closer to home. I am from Leicester, so I moved back to the Midlands. It was the best decision I made. My quality of life has improved; I will be able to buy a house shortly rather than flat sharing until I'm 45. I don't have to take the tube for an hour to get from East London to West London; I can drive around. I am just so much happier in the region. I find it friendlier and I find it more collegiate, so it was definitely the right decision for me.

NB: *Tell me a bit about the percentage of your time spent in court as compared with working at your desk?*

MJ: Usually I'm in court at least four, sometimes five, days a week. This week I had some personal things to deal with. I was only in court on Monday, and I took the rest of the week off to prep some trials and do some written advice. It's difficult to quantify. When I'm not in court, I am usually preparing for being in court.

NB: *I know some people who try to stick rigidly to an 8.30am to 5.00pm work pattern, but other people prefer working in the evenings.*

MJ: I am absolutely rubbish at organising to work only during the day. It probably would be far more conducive to having a healthy work-life balance, but I find that I work best ridiculously early or late in the day. That's the beauty of being self-employed, I can manage my time that way. I think that I would have really struggled with a 9-to-5 not just because that's not compatible with the way that I work but also because I suffer from anxiety and depression. I think being in one place from 9 to 5 and being dictated to about the times that I need to work would not be very helpful to me. I like working under pressure; I like working in my own time, I like managing my own time and I am capable of doing it. So as long as you're self-motivated and you do what you're supposed to when you're supposed to do it, there's a lot of freedom at the Bar in terms of how you work.

NB: *I agree with that. At the time I decided to study law, the one thing I knew about myself was that I didn't want to work at the same seat in the same desk in the same office, all day, every day, all the time. Being at the Bar is fabulous for that because it's the opposite. You go all sorts of places; one court one day, another court another day.*

MJ: Yes. I love it and I didn't really appreciate how much freedom I would have once I was at the Bar. Self-employment is something that actually really frightened me. I had always imagined being employed, having a regular pay cheque, having a pension, not having to do my own taxes, but now that I'm here, the pay-off is enormous because if I finish a hearing early and I've done all my prep, I will go out for the rest of the day and do what I want, or I will go have a nap. The freedom is great. There is no office politics. I don't have anyone telling me what to do and I don't have a manager that I have to constantly answer to. I am entirely in control of my practice, it's great!

NB: *What about the sorts of courts that you attend?*

MJ: I've been in court before magistrates right up to the High Court. I mostly see magistrates, district judges, circuit judges and part-time judges called recorders, and the bulk of my work is in the West Midlands. Occasionally, I have to go elsewhere, like London or Milton Keynes (the glamorous life I lead). I have been able to do work in courts that are further afield, like Manchester; because of remote hearings so I no longer have to travel to get there. It's given me a lot more freedom to not be limited to my geographical area.

NB: *The traditional wig and gown, would that be something that you would only wear in the High Court?*

MJ: In specific circumstances in the High Court and then in the Court of Appeal, but otherwise it's just business dress, all with a view to making things a bit more user-friendly in the Family Court and not intimidating.

NB: *Especially given that the number of litigants in person is increasing, I expect?*

MJ: Yes. In care proceedings, there is non-means tested, non-merits tested legal aid available for parents, which means that people tend not to represent themselves. I am against so many litigants in person in my private law matters, though, and it makes things more difficult. Obviously, the government was trying to make savings by cutting legal aid in those areas, but it's all a false economy because litigants in person, and this is no criticism of them, don't know what they are supposed to do, what the law is, they don't focus on the issues. We spend more time in court explaining things to them. They don't comply with directions, so there are delays. There are needless conflicts. An advocate will understand what is reasonable to fight over and what is something that you can just let go. It does make life difficult being against litigants in person, and obviously it must be a terrifying experience for them. I wouldn't want to navigate the court without a legal representative.

Some of the cases in which I have acted pro bono, had I not been there, my client would have had to do it alone. It's just a travesty because they are often very vulnerable, really distressed and they have to navigate law and procedure which is not straightforward. It's an impossible task to do well when unrepresented, and it just causes so much needless anxiety to everyone involved. And also, there is a really tricky ethical line because the advocate for the represented party is expected to assist the court in the administration of justice by helping the litigant in person where we can i.e. speaking to them ahead of time, trying to help them identify the issues, trying to help them articulate their position so we can communicate it to the judge. Obviously we can't advise them and it's a very, very, tricky ethical line to tread because you need to be helpful to them and to the court, but you also have to act fearlessly in your own client's interest. So, it just makes life difficult for everyone.

NB: *What sorts of your practice do you find the most interesting and also what areas do some people maybe find less interesting?*

MJ: All the areas of law are really interesting because they engage very different parts of my brain. Care proceedings are a totally different world to financial remedies and indeed to private children law. I am interested in lots of areas, for example the movement of children across borders and relocation, forced marriage, the interaction of family law with parallel immigration proceedings. I have just released a book with my colleague in Chambers on Practice Direction 12J which is the framework that we use to manage allegations of domestic abuse in the Family Court. I like that every day raises a new issue or a novel point of law that I haven't necessarily come across before. That's what keeps it exciting.

NB: *Has your time in practice matched or differed from expectations that you had when you were at Bar School?*

MJ: I had done so much work experience and so many mini-pupillages in family sets, so I think I had a relatively realistic idea of the realities of the job, like how much we wait around in court just to have the case come on and things like that. The only thing I hadn't really appreciated was the freedom of self-employment. In terms of whether Bar School prepared me for what came? Not really. I don't really recall much of what I did in Bar School. Whole chunks of it like civil and criminal litigation I never used and were never relevant ever again. As for witness examination, again, that was mostly in the criminal and civil context rather than in the family context. So, I think the minute I set foot in a court and was on my feet, everything I learnt in Bar School just flew out of my head and it's almost like you're back to square one and you are re-learning it.

With family law, I did one module in family litigation which was helpful. Conference skills, I use that quite a lot in practice so that was helpful. Like I said, the advocacy, and I don't know if this is necessarily a criticism of the Bar course, I just think that until you're there, it's difficult to really know what it's like. I did the pupils' advocacy course when I was doing pupillage and that was very, very rigorous. They used the Hampel method and would keep stopping you as you were speaking and correct you there and then rather than waiting until the end to give feedback and it's a pretty brutal process, but it does kick the bad habits out of you and you're getting feedback from these really eminent silks and judges, and I do think I learnt quite a lot from that.

NB: *What are the most difficult changes in your practice that you have had to get used to?*

MJ: I was only a tenant for four months before lockdown and then all of a sudden, my workload disappeared for about two or three months. It was pretty devastating financially but I'm very lucky because I live at home and I have financial support. I gave evidence about it to the Westminster Commission on the Sustainability of Legal Aid. I think between 23rd March and 8th June, I had about five legal aid cases; everything else was just adjourned en masse and I had practically nothing to do. When we are building up our reputation, junior practitioners obviously rely on senior barristers not being able to cover all the available work, but now if the solicitors' favoured barrister of 20 years' call is able to do hearings by video-link in Coventry in the morning and then in Wolverhampton in the afternoon, the solicitor will instruct the favoured barrister. There is no reason to instruct more junior counsel when the legal aid rate is going to be the same across the board. So, that was difficult, but my workload did come back to normal by the time the summer came round.

NB: *How would you describe your work-life balance?*

MJ: It's something I feel very strongly about. I think there is a culture of praising over-work at the Bar, feeling like it's a sign of competence or strength to never say no and to push yourself to the brink when you just burn out. Having this very serious mental health crisis in my pupillage year, which wasn't related to over-work I should say but was grounded in a whole host of different reasons, put things into perspective for me, and now I won't prioritise my work over my health. It's just not worth it. So I take on as much as I am able, and I have responded to e-mails that ask me to cover urgent hearings if I am able to do so, but I have no qualms telling my very supportive clerks and practice managers, like I did this week, that I am at capacity or I need some time off or I need more prep days. I have never received a negative response when I say I need a breather.

The beauty of being self-employed, like I said, is being able to manage your own practice, and I don't think enough barristers seem to recognise that or make the most of it. Barristers can feel as if they must do what their clerks tell them to do for fear of ending up on some blacklist and not receiving all the good work. That has not been my experience. A lot of the work-life balance issues are self-imposed. For instance, I took some holiday out in the summer, but I agreed to do a hearing during my holiday because my instructing solicitor wanted continuity of counsel. I had a week off planned, but I shifted it to a different week because there was a five-day trial that needed covering that I really wanted to do.

Part of the work-life balance issue is structural; it's the workload, the crowded court lists, court closures, backlog of work, Covid, last-minute briefs; but part of it is individual and I think it's a group of type A over-achievers who can't say no and want to do their best for their clients and then end up driving themselves into the ground.

NB: *When you're not in court, do you work in Chambers or at home?*

MJ: Home. I don't live in the West Midlands, and it takes me at least an hour to drive to Chambers. I love working from home so remote working worked out quite well for me. I do miss being around people in Chambers and being able to pick people's brains, but I always have a very long list of phone numbers of people that I need to call if I need help with something. I never feel detached from Chambers. At the very beginning of the pandemic they set up a system of wellbeing mentors so we each have someone in Chambers to talk to. I feel very supported in Chambers.

NB: *What is your view of how the Bar deals with wellbeing?*

MJ: It is great that we are talking more about wellbeing, but it's starting to become a bit of a corporate buzz word. People are talking about yoga sessions and going for a walk at lunchtime and non-uniform Fridays and all these other measures to improve wellbeing when there are so many structural issues that are impacting wellbeing like, particularly in crime, legal aid rates and over-work and bullying and harassment, sexual harassment, racism. I just worry that wellbeing becomes a tick-box exercise for many Chambers when it should be a constant process of reviewing procedures and seeing whether you're doing well enough and what can you do better. I've been co-organising a series for women in family law because I feel so strongly about it. It's called 'Welfare Wednesdays' because I was so fed up of the term 'wellbeing'. The aim is to address what we think are the real hard-hitting issues that are affecting our collective mental health. The first session was on overcoming rejection timed to coincide with pupillage offer day, and it's all about developing resilience. We've also done sessions on navigating the barrister-clerk relationship and family law supervision. I think wellbeing is a very multi-faceted issue and I'm worried that it's being watered down and the approach to it can be quite reductive.

NB: *How techy is your practice area?*

MJ: My Chambers has just gone paperless, though I was always pretty paperless anyway. My Mac is the only thing I ever really take around with me. I avoid having paper bundles. I live in perpetual fear of leaving a bundle on the train and having to report myself to the Information Commissioner's Office, so I prefer being paperless. I was introduced to a PDF expert during the paperless working sessions that were being run by the Family Law Bar Association: game-changer! I now annotate and bookmark my electronic bundles beautifully. I have an app on my phone that scans, so I rarely need to go into Chambers or use my home scanner. I store my receipts electronically on an app so that I can send them to my accountant.

NB: *When I first started out at the Bar back in 2000, big heavy trolley cases were the thing because you'd have folders and files and your Blackstone's or your Archbold in heavy copy. It was back-breaking work!*

MJ: I do have my Red Book in hardcopy which mostly I carry around for show, but I think the era of barristers trekking around the Royal Courts of Justice with suitcases is long gone or on its way out. I will say that technology has created this expectation of being constantly available. I had my work e-mails on my phone, and it was causing me so much stress because it was the first thing I read when I wake up in the morning. I deleted my work account from my phone and I have to actually log in to my e-mails and onto my laptop to access it, and I think that when we use technology this much, you do have to set those kinds of boundaries otherwise you are just constantly 'on'.

NB: *Before you started the job, did you have any expectations about travelling?*

MJ: I knew that there was a lot of travel involved but I don't think I really appreciated how much that would fatigue me. In practice, before I was driving, I'd have to get a train to Birmingham and then get another train to whichever court I was going to, so door-to-door, it would usually take about two hours. Four hours round trip travel on top of a full day of court and then you get home and start working on your papers for the next day. It is exhausting to do that five days a week, so I was very happy with remote working. I enjoy going into court when I have to go into court. I like seeing the court staff who I know by name; I like seeing my friends and colleagues, I like the experience of going to court but to not have to do that every day has actually been a massive relief because I don't live on circuit.

NB: *Have you any experiences or observations about diversity at the Bar?*

MJ: The Bar is not diverse. It's not a meritocracy either. It's a very old institution with very old, ingrained prejudices that is going to take a very long time to dislodge. I had a work experience student who said to me that she hadn't seen many other people who looked like me on the profiles of Chambers' websites – that had been my experience as well. I have been very fortunate in that the Chambers where I did pupillage and the Chambers that I'm currently at are, relatively speaking, quite diverse but that's not true of the rest of the Bar. I don't see a lot of people who look like me at the Bar. I say to people that my face shouldn't be an encouraging statistic for diversity at the Bar because yes, I'm brown, but I am also privately educated, middle class, very privileged, went to an elite university; I was not the first person in my family to go to university either, so for all these reasons I was boosted up to the Bar by a system that was built to advantage me. So, I think there's a lot of work to be done, and I would encourage people to look critically at any statistics that seem to suggest that the Bar is more diverse than it is because there is more lurking underneath. I boost the BME statistics but that's not necessarily reflective of what's going on under the surface.

NB: *Can you give me an idea of the sort of income progression that's typical in the early years of practice in family law?*

MJ: I think between pupillage and my first year of tenancy, it took a little bit of time to get an income stream going and I don't think enough people appreciate that. My pupillage award was relatively generous but I was living in London so I would blow through it quite easily. As you start doing work, there is a lag in the fees coming through to you, so you have to hope that you have very efficient fees clerks who are chasing after your money to ensure that you're getting paid. Even so, it takes a while for legal aid to filter through. I did a case in January last year and I was paid over a year later. I remember chasing my clerks and going 'what case is this about' because I had completely forgotten about it.

My fees have increased quite significantly, comparing my first year's accounts against my second year. I have a solid income which will likely continue to rise with seniority. I think it's good to have a diverse practice of both legal aid and private work if you can get it because a lot of the work that I do on my legal aid cases isn't remunerated, whereas my fees for my privately paid work are negotiated by my clerks with the view to agreeing a fee which is considered appropriate for the work that I'm doing and the level of seniority that I'm at.

NB: *Any thoughts about the future of the family bar?*

MJ: You are never going to run out of interesting work. I also don't think that family legal aid is as low as criminal legal aid so I think that if you are worried about surviving at the family bar, the same concerns that you might have about the criminal bar are not so acute at the family bar, particularly if you diversify like I said by doing private work as well. I'm hoping that the remote working that we embraced during Covid is here to stay for directions hearings and things like that because it's really not necessary to go into court to travel hours for a five-minute mention. I hope that we can be a bit more efficient because there is a huge court backlog as well, and we will hopefully be able to cut through it more, but I do think that face-to-face hearings are often important. I think that family law is a people-based job; you need to look people in the eye and give them advice they don't necessarily want to hear, and you have to show compassion and empathy and that can't be replicated by a bot or by a virtual service. So, I think that there is a role for technology, but it needs to be very carefully managed alongside what makes the family bar human.

There is also a narrowing of the line between barristers and solicitors. I am public access qualified so I can be instructed directly by members of the public and I'm often against solicitors and legal executives who are doing their own advocacy. The strict distinction between the Bar and solicitors, particularly in family law, is becoming very thin.

But I do worry that family lawyers are at breaking point. I worry that particularly in care proceedings there is so much work to be done and so little time. Everyone is at capacity. There are huge existing delays in the system because of things like court closures which were exacerbated by Covid, and there is going to be a wellbeing crisis in the very near future I suspect, and what I worry about is that there is going to be a brain drain and a total re-directing of talent from this area of practice.

NB: *Do you mean as barristers turn to other areas of law instead or turn to other jobs even?*

MJ: Both. I think particularly in legal aid work. I think some barristers will just think this isn't worth it. There are other areas of law that are more lucrative. I also think that the legal profession as a whole is exhausted. We come into the profession with skills that are appealing in other professions so it gives us a lot of options. There needs to be more investment in keeping people in the profession because we can just take our skills elsewhere. Not me, anytime soon. I'm happy where I am but I don't have caring responsibilities; I don't have any dependents. I can afford to not have a life; I can manage the unpredictable lifestyle. The only person that I'm irritating is my boyfriend. I honestly don't know how I could manage it if I did have kids. I am in awe of people who have kids or caring responsibilities because I don't know how they manage their time with such an unpredictable diary as well.

2 Commercial Chancery

An Interview with Ted Loveday, Maitland Chambers

NB: *Ted, when did you begin tenancy and what areas of law have you practised in since beginning tenancy?*

TL: My tenancy at Maitland Chambers began in September 2017. The typical practice at my Chambers is often described as 'commercial chancery' which can be quite a confusing term. In reality it covers a large range of different areas of law, and it can vary between different sets of Chambers, so it's important to break it down. In terms of my practice at Maitland, first, I see a lot of commercial litigation – disputes between businesses, breaches of contract, civil fraud, cases relating to finance transactions and so on, and this makes up a major chunk of my work. I have also practised insolvency, company and some property law, and I have a personal interest in charity law. There are huge overlaps between these areas.

If students are interested in anything which might broadly be described as 'commercial chancery', I think it's important for them to drill down into exactly what areas of work appeal to them. For example, the expression 'chancery' can be associated with some other areas such as trusts, tax, probate and Court of Protection work, but I don't have a particular interest in those areas.

NB: *Did you always want to go to the commercial bar?*

TL: No – in fact, I didn't always want to go into law! I actually started out studying history at university. By the end of my degree, I had switched to studying law out of curiosity. I was good at it and enjoyed it, so I decided to have a go and see what it was like as a career. Eventually I got a pupillage at my current Chambers and I have had a great time, but it's very much been a series of discoveries.

DOI: 10.4324/9781003111597-3

NB: *Did you have to do the GDL [the Graduate Diploma in Law, or conversion course]?*

TL: No, as I studied all the necessary modules in my degree.

NB: *Can you give some examples of cases you are in right now?*

TL: Of course! I do a mix of smaller cases on my own – where you might be in and out of court quite regularly – and larger, longer-running ones with other barristers. To give an example of the bigger cases, today I've been working on a case in the Commercial Court which I'm doing with Edmund Cullen QC, one of my colleagues in Maitland Chambers. The case is about the relationship between different parties who were financing a film. A whole series of things went wrong during the production process and the film was never properly released. This meant everyone who had put money into the film were fighting over who should bear the losses. Like many commercial cases, it involves rival interpretations of a series of contracts and examination of the actual interactions between the people who were involved in the project. The court will very much have to trace what when wrong, why it went wrong, when it went wrong and who is responsible for that.

NB: *And while they are all arguing about who bears the losses, they are all spending more money to determine that question?*

TL: Exactly. The dispute is over £2 or £3 million pounds which sounds like a lot – but by Commercial Court standards, it's relatively small. It's important for all of us to make sure that our clients are getting good value for money and not spending disproportionate amounts on it. At the moment we are in the middle of disclosure, which involves going through thousands and thousands of e-mails that the parties exchanged several years ago to make sure that the other side has access to the evidence they need. The e-mails have to be read by someone who is legally qualified and that's a classic example of where you have got to be careful to keep the costs within reasonable bounds.

NB: *You talked about the odd ten-minute cases where you are in and out? What sorts of things might they be?*

TL: As I say, it's good to have a mix of bigger and smaller cases. At my Chambers I would say the bread-and-butter hearings for unled juniors include smaller commercial cases, insolvency and property hearings.

Starting with insolvency, this can be a good source of advocacy practice because there are a lot more hearings than in typical commercial cases. For example, when you have a client that wants to wind up a company – that means put it into liquidation – this may involve going to court several times before you can achieve that, especially if the company can persuade the judge that it's going to be able to pay you.

One of the odd things about insolvency for me is that it's one of the very few areas where I get to wear a wig and gown – or at least it was before virtual hearings started. Traditionally, all applications to put companies into liquidation would be heard at the same time as part of a long list, perhaps 100 or more companies at once, during the same hearing once a week – described as the 'companies winding up list' or informally the 'winders'. You would have several dozen junior barristers representing the various companies and their creditors, crowded into a single courtroom wearing their robes and finery, and each company would get about 30 seconds to explain why they shouldn't be wound up. You get last-minute surprises and a lot of adjournments because the judge is often going to want to give everyone a second chance to pay, but ultimately it can be quite brutal too because it all happens so fast. It's a good chance to get on your feet and get used to the sound of your own voice in court. This is important for commercial practitioners in particular, as opportunities for oral advocacy aren't as common as they are at other parts of the Bar.

On the property side, a typical hearing at early stages might be a possession hearing. The tenant falls behind with rent or there is some other reason that the landlord wants to get rid of the tenant. You are either trying to obtain a possession order, or – if you're on the tenant's side – trying to buy more time or stay for as long as possible. Those can start with very straightforward, short hearings where there isn't that much to be said on each side, but you'd be surprised by how often it raises complicated issues and of course it can be emotionally charged. Other issues might include disrepair if the landlord isn't keeping the property in a good state, if there are leaks, vermin and so on. I have seen all kinds of terrible things that go wrong with housing, and it can be very satisfying helping tenants to get them sorted.

NB: *Thank you, Ted. Can you tell me about the sorts of tasks that you have had to do in those sorts of cases?*

TL: I do a lot of drafting and a lot of written work and a lot of written Advice. Obviously, that doesn't mean to say there is no oral advocacy; there is plenty, but it is fair to say that I practise at a more paper-focused end of the Bar. I will very often be asked to draft pleadings, so all of the skills you build at Bar School in that area are helpful. Obviously, you do formal written Advices as well at all stages of cases, but I will often be asked to advise by e-mail – these days it's not always a traditional, formal set of instructions saying, 'Advice from Counsel'. You can advise in conference as well; that happens a lot.

One thing that you don't really learn at Bar School is the more informal aspect of being involved as part of a team on an on-going case. For example, it is very, very common indeed for civil and commercial barristers to be involved in drafting letters for your instructing solicitors to send to the other side – either writing them from scratch or commenting on a draft prepared by the solicitors. You have to get all the right content in, make it short and persuasive. The primary goal is to persuade the other side to agree to something you are asking them to do, but if they don't agree, the letter may end up in front of the judge so you will need draft all letters with a view to ultimately persuading the judge that your client's position is reasonable. So you do a lot of drafting and re-drafting of letters. You might also be involved in witness statements and other documents – again, this isn't something you do much at Bar School, but you are often brought in to help on them, regardless of the size of the case. Back in the olden days, I suppose letters and solicitors were treated as 'solicitors' jobs' – but the profession has changed a lot and you will definitely be expected to roll up your sleeves and help with them.

NB: *From a criminal lawyer's perspective, when you think about a barrister drafting witness statements, you think 'that sounds so wrong!' but of course, it isn't at all in particular areas of law.*

TL: Yes! Actually, you are taught in Bar School that there are important ethical rules about when you should and shouldn't draft witness statements. Those rules are still important because you have to maintain your independence. If you're drafting a statement for a witness whose credibility is going to be an issue, you do need to stop and think about it – because you don't want to get pulled into being part of that debate personally. Having said this, with civil witness statements, it is much rarer for the witness's honesty to be called into question and so solicitors are often keener to get counsel involved in helping with them. The main reason for this is that solicitors generally appreciate your role as part of the team and will frequently want to have you involved in helping with them to make sure the evidence is as helpful and persuasive as possible. After all, you are going to be the person who has to argue the case at trial so it's important for you to be happy with the materials you're working with. I should add that it may still be the case that a witness's credibility is an issue – especially in fraud or hotly contested commercial cases. In those cases, you need to be especially circumspect about your role in the drafting of evidence, but you may still be involved in some capacity. Often, the junior/senior relationship helps smooth that over – the junior might get a little more stuck into the preparation of evidence because ultimately it is going to be the silk who is doing the cross-examining at trial.

NB: *There must be a lot of negotiation as well with your opponents, I guess?*

TL: Yes. We definitely do a lot of negotiation. That starts with advising on offers to be made. Sometimes you need to tell the client to take a tougher position, but frankly it's common for you to find yourself urging your clients to push for settlement. People from outside the legal world don't always appreciate quite how hideous and expensive litigation is going to be. I can see you nodding from your experience in your own area?

NB: *Sometimes it's really hard work isn't it, to make your client understand the severity of the risk that he or she might be proposing to you, and you have really got to calm things down sometimes and say, look, here's the reality of it, your choice, but here are the risks.*

TL: Exactly. It happens a lot.

NB: *We have talked about the winding-up lists that you might do, but what other sort of advocacy might someone in the first couple of years maybe in your field expect to do?*

TL: I have done my share of applications of different sorts in the County Court; might be half a day, might be a day: summary judgment, setting aside default judgment, setting aside orders of various different kinds, civil procedure skirmishes of different types. I have done small claims trials, fast track and multi-track trials. There are also insolvency applications of various kinds, as well as property cases in the County Court or the High Court. Then at the other end of the scale a commercial or chancery junior will have plenty of opportunities to act as part of a larger team in bigger cases often in the High Court – although you don't have the same level of responsibility, the cases can be much more interesting, and you get to work with some really talented people. It's good to get a balance of both.

NB: *Is mediation something that you get involved with?*

TL: Yes. I love taking part in mediations. The role of a barrister at a mediation is slightly odd as it's not clearly defined. In theory, you are there to give the legal perspective, to advise on the overall strategy, and to be a sounding-board if the client asks, 'what's the risk if I don't accept this offer?', or 'how much do you think my claim is worth?' You are very much there to get everyone to see the strength of your case.

NB: *What sorts of cases have you had that have come before a mediator?*

TL: I have had contract cases, so effectively, civil, commercial-type cases where businesses fall out over money. A common area where mediations can be successful are company and partnership-type cases where business partners have fallen out; that's exceptionally common and there are all kinds of court cases that that can lead to and involving different areas of law. Deep down, the human problem is the same: people who thought they trusted each other, but the relationship has broken down and now the only result is that they get their lawyers involved.

NB: *You're quite right. That goes across all fields of law because it is the root of many problems in family law isn't it, as well, and also in crime?*

TL: Absolutely. When people start a big new project together, whether that is a business or buying a property or starting a family, they assume that they will always get on. They rarely stop and think, 'what if it goes wrong?' If they did, they could have spent a few hundred quid on drafting a proper agreement and avoided trouble down the line. But unless you're a lawyer you usually don't think like this. So it can be sad when effectively the shared asset, whatever it is, starts being frittered away on lawyers' fees. In those cases, both sides' lawyers are usually trying to persuade their clients to go to mediation, saying, 'look, this is your chance to draw a line under it'.

NB: *What sorts of people or organisations have largely been your clients?*

TL: It is a mix of individuals and professionals of some sort – businesses, charities, government bodies and other organisations. Disputes between two businesses or organisations will usually have some sort of personal side. But this is more common in disputes involving private individuals, especially where there is a real human issue at the heart of it. Those cases can be the most satisfying even if they're not always the most prestigious.

NB: *What's your caseload been like and how has it compared with your second six or your first six?*

TL: In terms of how my practice has developed since I started out, I'd say there have been three broad changes. First, there have been shifts in terms of areas of law, as I've picked up an interest in charity law and have spent a great deal of time on pro bono work in a range of areas which might be less typical for my set of Chambers. Second, I applied for a role as a judicial assistant working closely with judges – it has been a really interesting insight into how the system works, and hopefully will be something I can use to develop my practice in new directions. The third change, I would say, is that over time I've built up connections with solicitors who I enjoy working with, and this has led to more and more interesting cases through those personal relationships.

You mentioned a second six, but in fact it's common at the commercial bar and the chancery bar to have no real distinction between the first and second six of pupillage. Certainly in my case, the whole of my 12 months' pupillage was devoted to training and assessment, and I wasn't sent out on my feet until the start of my tenancy. I can't speak for every Chambers, but it is common in these areas for much of your efforts during pupillage to be focused on getting good at the paperwork side of things – that's because paperwork is such an important aspect of the practice – although there are often workshops and courses to keep your oral advocacy skills sharp.

This means the start of your tenancy is very different from pupillage because you will be doing hearings for the first time – that's obviously stimulating and challenging.

NB: *It couldn't be more opposite than a criminal or common law pupillage, I guess, could it?*

TL: I had friends who were obviously doing crime and other areas of law and especially in my year group. In some ways we were both jealous of each other! They were often stressed at having to appear in the Magistrates Court five or six days a week, being thrown in at the deep end with some really tough cases, and they wished they could have some of the more detailed tuition and support that I was getting back in Chambers. On the other hand, I was still sitting at a desk reading and typing away or shadowing people, rather than doing cases of my own – and it's fair to say that sometimes I was really stir-crazy and wanted to get going myself.

NB: *How much of your time is spent, would you say, in courts or tribunals and how much at your desk?*

TL: I would say less than 20% in court, so about one day a week. That varies because some weeks there are no hearings at all, and other weeks you might be having hearings over several days or even the occasional bigger trial running over several weeks. There are all kinds of different sets in our area of commercial chancery, but the balance of work at my

Chambers, because it involves insolvency and property work as well as commercial work, involves some more opportunities to have your own hearings as a junior. We've already discussed those, and that work actually is quite good fun as a junior, and it does mean you get out there and get some advocacy experience on your own and in small hearings. I have several friends who are practicing in what might be described as 'pure' commercial sets of Chambers, which can be frustrating because the juniors do very little advocacy at all. They might be involved in several huge cases at once, but on each of them they will be the most junior person in a large team. So if you have an insolvency element or a property element to your Chambers, or some other area of practice, you are likely to get to do little more advocacy as the junior than if you do purely commercial work. I know that this is actually a long-term worry in our areas of the Bar, because there's a concern that the younger generation may not be getting enough advocacy experience as they work their way up through the system.

NB: *Can we discuss a little more the courts or tribunals that you do attend. Obviously it isn't going to be the Crown Court, I bet you have never been in a Crown Court.*

TL: I don't think so, unfortunately, although I have been in the Magistrates' Court a couple of times! Not for criminal cases, but there are a small number of civil cases which might find their way into the Magistrates' Court – for example, applications by local councils to recover unpaid business rates.

The vast majority of my cases are either in the High Court or the County Court. County Court hearings generally have a value under £100,000 and they could be anywhere in the country. High Court hearings could involve anything really – there is huge variety. Most of my High Court work will be in the parts of the High Court known as the Business and Property Courts, which include the Commercial Court and the Insolvency and Companies Court. Appeals from the High Court may end up going to the Court of Appeal and ultimately the Supreme Court. I've also done work in the Administrative Court and various tribunals. Most hearings in these courts require business suits, so we don't wear robes. The few hearings where I might use robes would be the winding-up petitions that we've talked about; most appeals; and contempt of court hearings.

Contempt of court usually arises in cases involving injunctions. It might be a fraud case, a contract case or a property case. Say the judge has made a freezing injunction where the defendant's assets are frozen to stop them making off with their assets. If the claimant has evidence that the defendant has breached the injunction, they can make an application to commit them for contempt of court, that is, either to have the defendant fined or sent to prison because they disobeyed the court order. Because the liberty of the subject is at stake, these hearings require robes to send a message about the seriousness of the occasion. I have a contempt hearing coming up in Nottingham soon, so that will be a rare time when I need to pack up my wig and gown for a hearing outside London. Most of my robed hearings have been in London because that's where most winding-up hearings take place.

NB: *Why is it that most winding-up hearings are in London?*

TL: The default is that the cases are heard in London because that's where the biggest insolvency specialism is – both among the Bar and the judiciary – but the courts are very much trying to localise the hearings at the moment when they are tied to a particular region of the UK.

NB: *What sorts of areas of your practice do you find the most interesting and which areas do some people maybe find less interesting?*

TL: I enjoy working with clients – especially clients who are less familiar with the legal system – to try to understand their needs, to build up a relationship with them and to help them navigate the unfamiliar world of litigation. I like also the problem-solving aspect of my job. That's something that you get a lot of in the sort of cases that I do. Obviously, in commercial litigation, you are in a practical world and you need to understand the practical needs of your clients, but at the same time you do get to grips with some knotty and quite abstract legal problems. I also really love being on my feet, I love the advocacy; but if you need to do that every day of the week, this the wrong area for you because it is more paper-based.

NB: *That's really interesting because the clinical negligence practitioner who I spoke to made a vital point: when you're at Bar School, there is a tendency sometimes for a student to focus on 'what area of law would I enjoy the most'; whereas she thought the better question to ask is, 'looking at my skillset, what am I good at'. Subtle emphasis, but very important I think.*

TL: I think you need to think about what skills you most enjoy using. What do you want your typical day to look like? Do you like the sound of going to Chambers and thinking about strategy and advising on the clients' legal problems, or do you want to be going out to court and examining witnesses and speaking up for your clients? Perhaps you like both, but you need to think about what balance between them you want to get. When I speak to students and mini-pupils about this, generally I'll tell them that the only way to find out what you like is by getting exposure to it – mini-pupillages, working as a paralegal and volunteering are all good ways of testing things out.

NB: *We talked about you being led and the sorts of tasks you have to do when you are led in bigger cases, but would it be useful just to talk about the sort of actual tasks that you have done to help your leader in different cases?*

TL: Each leader has their own demands and their own ways of working – unfortunately, when you become a QC, you don't get trained in how to lead a junior, which is why there's so much variety! When you get instructed to work alongside a leader, the first thing you should do is talk to your leader about how they work and what they expect of you. Some leaders are delegators, and they will expect you to prepare all the materials before they even touch the case, and they will then look over it briefly and hopefully approve what you've prepared for them. Others will want to be completely over the papers first, so they can prepare a document themselves, and they'll just rely on you to fill in some gaps here and there, or to carry out specific bits of research. When it comes to hearings and cross-examination there will also be a range of different tasks you might be asked to do. It varies hugely between silks and between other people you are working with.

In general, your work when you are led will very often involve making the first draft of things and being on top of documents and tasks for them. You might be drafting grounds of appeal, skeleton arguments, perhaps doing witness statements. When you are instructed to give Advice, again, it varies hugely. You might get silks who want to take complete ownership of the Advice and do all the work themselves and they're not comfortable with something where you have done the legwork. Others will leave you to take a lot of the initiative. It's fun getting a mix of different types of leaders. It is really fun when you have a silk who pays huge attention to detail and gets stuck in alongside you but, equally, it can be quite flattering if you prepare a long skeleton argument and it gets signed off and adopted by somebody senior with very few changes.

NB: *Ted, looking back, do you think that the sort of work you did at Bar School prepared you for what you have ended up doing in this first year or two?*

TL: Some of it did, some of it didn't. I found the training in drafting, oral and written advocacy really useful. I've also often drawn on what I learned during the alternative dispute resolution part of the Bar course – we did a mock mediation which was actually pretty realistic and has stood me in good stead for real ones. You might be surprised that I'm also glad to have studied criminal litigation. A lot of people think that by the time they get to Bar School, they know what they want to do and so it's a waste of time, but I think it did create some collegiality – you know what other areas members of the Bar practise in. If you call yourself a barrister, you should have some general idea of how each part of the legal system works.

On the other hand, the civil litigation course was dreary because it basically involved large amounts of rote-learning of the civil procedure rules which you were expected to regurgitate in the exam word-for-word. And you would be marked down if you got the wording slightly wrong. Obviously you need to know the outline of how the rules work, but I'm not sure rote-learning the White Book is a sensible use of anyone's time.

I found much of the Bar course useful, although of course I have some criticisms and it's fair to say I learned far more during pupillage than I did during the Bar course.

NB: *But maybe Bar School gave you a base from which you could make much better use of pupillage?*

TL: Potentially – especially with the drafting and advocacy training which I mentioned. I know the contents of the course have changed a lot since I did it, and I can't speak for the course as it stands today, so it might be that some of the rote-learning has gone.

NB: *When you look back do you think, I'm glad I took certain subject options at university rather than something else?*

TL: I am definitely glad I studied contract law properly in an academic setting, as it's extremely useful for what I do on a day-to-day basis. Oddly, the lecturers would often apologise that the details about contract law won't be useful in practice because it involves quite abstract questions such as whether a contract actually exists, or whether there has been consideration. It's fair to say that these questions aren't very important for most lawyers. For example, if you're a conveyancing solicitor, there's rarely ever going to be any doubt about whether a contract exists or not. But these sorts of questions do actually become important in commercial litigation. You get real controversy about issues like whether there is consideration or what test for remoteness you use. So paying attention in contract lectures definitely helped me at the Bar.

There were some optional subjects that I really enjoyed, even if they don't directly apply in my practice today. I did a wonderful course called Law and Development in my final year which was all about the relationship between the legal system and economic development. For example, we studied a lot of efforts by the World Bank on how to improve the rule of law in developing countries. Does it work? It is sometimes colonialist? Are there problems with it? It gave a really interesting perspective on law around the world beyond the black letter stuff.

In terms of advice to students, I would say, do the essential mandatory courses that you have to do but otherwise, pick what takes your fancy. You might be spending a long time in your chosen area of practice; you will have plenty of time to learn the legal detail, but this is your chance to really expand your horizons. I am a big advocate for doing options which some people might say are less 'useful' in the real world because now is the time to be intellectually curious.

NB: *I completely agree with that. Can you tell me about the most difficult changes you have had to get used to as you have made your way through the first couple of years of your tenancy?*

TL: Managing your practice is something no-one ever trains you in. Although you will hopefully have support from your clerks, your pupil supervisors and your colleagues, it's important to realise that ultimately you are responsible for what happens in your career. You might be encouraged to go in particular directions and, even if you're not, it's quite easy to get caught up in one case after another and start drifting without thinking about your direction. Where do you want to be going? What are your goals?

On a more mundane level, it's crucial to manage your time properly, and an important part of this is learning how to say 'no'. Hopefully you will have lots of people who want to instruct you, but you need to stop and think whether you can actually fit the case in. Some barristers never get their work-life balance quite right because they're terrified to turn away instructions and they end up agreeing to everything. But my view is that ultimately you need to learn that you can't work all the hours in the day and you need to decide what balance you want to strike. Nobody else is going to do this for you, so you need to take responsibility for it.

NB: *This brings us on to the work-life balance. First, when you are not in court and you are working at your computer, do you do it in Chambers or at home?*

TL: Currently, I am working at home. Even before the lockdown, barristers with a more commercial or chancery practice had the opportunity to work from home more than most due to the relatively large proportion of your work that involves reading, writing and drafting. Many of my colleagues would spend some of their time working from home, especially those with children or family commitments. If your work is not primarily court-based, there is a lot of flexibility, and this is definitely set to increase now that working from home has been normalised.

I think it's still important to come into Chambers when you can, to make sure that you're bonding with your colleagues and keeping some sort of collegiate atmosphere. Many sets of Chambers, including my own, try to encourage this by holding various social events. In bigger cases you get a lot more social contact because you will be working with a team of solicitors and often other barristers. But equally you do need to be happy working on your own sometimes, since there will always be cases where you're essentially sitting with your papers or your PDFs and ploughing through them and producing a product at the end of that.

NB: *Do you have your own room in Chambers?*

TL: Yes. Up until recently everyone in my Chambers had their own room. We have now, in the last year or so, adopted the policy of moving over towards sharing space sometimes – which is sensible if people are working from home a lot. There is no point in renting a building full of empty space, so we are increasingly sharing two people to a room.

NB: *Does that work?*

TL: Yes. Personally I am quite sociable, and I'd be glad to share a space. I know that views on this differ between barristers, though.

NB: *How techy are the practice areas that you work in?*

TL: Things have changed in recent years, but today pretty much everyone can have a completely paperless practice most of the time if they want to.

NB: *In crime we started off with the digital system. All the prosecution evidence is on a central system that judges, advocates and solicitors could all see. That's made a magnificent difference. It's been developed further into the 'common platform'. I would like to be utterly paperless. If I can just take my MacBook to court, I'm happy. In your area of law, it's pretty techy too?*

TL: Yes, although pre-lockdown you would still have trials with walls and walls of bundles, with reams and reams of paper flying around. Even if everyone had a laptop in court, there would still be walls of bundles. I think you will still have barristers who will want to have their paper, if anything as a comfort blanket, but you can work without it if you want. I had a real-world physical hearing in the Midlands two or three weeks ago. It was liberating because, before lockdown, when I went out of London I'd be breaking my back with a wheelie case full of papers. You really feel it taking a physical toll when you get home in the evening. But this time, I just took a rucksack with a laptop and a charger. I was terrified the technology would fail on me, but it was a huge relief not to lug all those papers up and down the country. You have to get used to some other things – like I didn't know where to hold the laptop when I was making submissions and I had to find the right place to perch it so that it could still be connected to the charger in court. But once you get over those teething problems, it's great.

NB: *So is the way you run your practice job less paper-based, and more digital?*

TL: I am at the more digital end of the spectrum. I don't like to accumulate ring binders. The only exception is if I've been staring at a screen all day and need a fresh perspective on what I've been drafting, I'll sometimes print it out and mark it up in red ink. But even this is quite rare for me now, because I don't have a printer at home!

NB: *What would you say are your typical hours of work are?*

TL: Probably around half nine to half six. I am not sure there are typical hours of work because on a busy day, it could be a lot more than that. But I like to try and keep boundaries between work and not work.

NB: *From what you've said you probably don't do that much travelling, do you?*

TL: No, most of my work is in London. I might go outside London when I have cases in courts in different parts of the country, or sometimes to meet solicitors or attend mediations. Because travelling is not that common, it's quite fun – you get a change of scene and the chance to explore towns and cities in different parts of the country.

NB: *Were your expectations about that accurate?*

TL: I think they were. I knew what I was getting in for.

NB: *How do you find the work-life balance in your fields of law? Is your experience the same as your contemporaries that you keep in touch with who might be in other areas of law?*

TL: I think with civil work, if you're a workaholic and you want to do lots of cases and probably if you're very ambitious, you can end up working very long hours. Some people have the perception that if you want to impress clients and solicitors you need to work very long hours. You will certainly be working long hours if you are keen to take on a lot of big cases at once.

On the other hand, it is possible to learn to say 'no' to work and set your own expectations for what sort of balance you want. It depends on what your goals are. There will always be stressful cases and there will still be last-minute work that needs doing, but over the years I have become better at predicting what my workload is going to be like and working out what I can afford to take on.

Another important part of getting your work-life balance right is communicating with your colleagues effectively. You need to make it clear to your solicitors and leaders what sort of hours you work, when you are going to be on holiday and so on. Although litigation can be demanding, people will ultimately understand that you want to have a life outside work. The trick is talking to people openly about it and making sure that you've agreed a way of getting your work done in good time. Most sets of Chambers are very supportive of welfare and there are people you can talk to – there will be avenues for troubleshooting.

NB: *Coming to the end now. Next question is about diversity at the Bar because we are keen to know about, insofar as people want to talk about them, any experiences of sex equality, race equality, social mobility and any other areas that you think might touch on the topic of diversity are. Just whether you have anything to say about it?*

TL: It's a difficult topic. It's the number one problem facing the Bar. I'm not sure I'm much of an authority on these issues, but of course of course they deeply bother me, and I think most of my colleagues. As a set of Chambers, we make big efforts to recruit from diverse groups and we contribute to outreach and mentoring schemes, but obviously the Bar still has a long way to go.

NB: *Is there anything you can say about income progression in the areas of law that you do, perhaps over the early years of practice so before your stage and beyond your stage?*

TL: The problem is that this varies massively between individual barristers, even within the same areas of practice! I can only speak for myself, and I'm lucky to be practising in the area that I am because it is relatively financially stable. I think it's fair to say that, although there may be cashflow issues in the first year or two, civil and commercial barristers end up with substantial earnings by most people's standards.

I think the Bar Council publishes statistics on this if students are interested in finding average figures.

NB: *That's great. And we are finally onto the last question is just whether you have any thoughts about the future of the Bar in your areas?*

TL: That's a big question.

NB: *Criminal practitioners have a lot to say to me about that, and even those who work in personal injury, too, because there are some changes on the horizon there, maybe in commercial, chancery, maybe not a lot has changed and not a lot will change?*

TL: I don't think that there is a fear that the commercial bar is dying or declining. When I was applying for pupillages, one of the common interview questions was whether we might be heading towards a fused profession, or a world where solicitors want to do it all themselves. Actually, it turns out that specialist courtroom advocates are still in demand and still will be in demand for a good while. Of course, we need to be alert to how things are developing – especially with the move towards virtual hearings and digitisation. But I think the civil bar will survive and do well, and if anything we have a responsibility for looking out for the rest of the Bar because there are certainly bigger threats facing our criminal and family law colleagues.

3 Civil, Personal Injury, Clinical Negligence

An Interview with Rebecca Titus-Cobb, St John's Buildings Chambers

NB: *When did you start tenancy, Rebecca?*

RTC: My tenancy started in October 2018 at St John's Buildings in Manchester, just after my 12 months' pupillage had finished.

NB: *I'd like to begin with looking at what areas of law you've been practising in and whether you always wanted to go into those fields?*

RTC: I practise in civil law across a fairly broad range of areas including personal injury, clinical negligence and inquests. I am also starting to develop a Court of Protection practice. My practice is varied but is increasingly focused on actions against public bodies and work which has a civil liberties or public law element to it.

I have always had an interest in cases which raise interesting ethical, medico-legal and moral issues, particularly those cases where the rights and interests of individuals and the state can come into conflict. Before coming to the Bar, my ambition was to do work with a civil liberties or public law element, so I am happy that my practice does incorporate these areas.

I think it is important to recognise that if your interests lie in more niche areas of law, it may be that you develop a practice which is broad but encompasses those specialised fields. Personally, I perhaps do more personal injury work than I may have initially planned to, but I enjoy the work and it complements the other areas of my practice.

NB: *Is this where you always intended to be?*

RTC: That is a difficult question to answer because I think that there is a gap between expectations of practice areas and the reality of actually working in those practice areas. Once you start pupillage, and actually experience the work, preconceptions about practice areas probably

DOI: 10.4324/9781003111597-4

change. When I undertook the GDL and the Bar course, I didn't necessarily understand how the areas which I was interested in would manifest in reality and what kind of work would be available to me at an early stage in my career. I knew that other areas of law, criminal and family for instance, were not necessarily for me and so to that extent, I always intended to have a civil practice. However, I probably did not fully appreciate that the kind of cases and issues which I was interested in as a student arise in a wide variety of practice areas.

NB: *You practise in a few different areas of law; how would you describe the split between them all?*

RTC: The split has changed during the course of my pupillage and now into tenancy. At the start of pupillage and in my first year of tenancy I was doing a greater percentage of general civil and personal injury work including road traffic cases, accidents at work and public liability cases. This still makes up a large part of my practice. I would say that classic personal injury work still makes up around 50% of my practice, with the other areas, including inquests, clinical negligence and Court of Protection making up the other 50%.

NB: *Is road traffic work about people who have just come by injuries in road traffic accidents?*

RTC: Yes, it includes those cases where an injury has occurred as a result of a road traffic accident but also those cases where there are no injuries suffered but issues remain as to liability and other losses flowing from the accident. The bulk of small claims cases which you will come across as a junior civil practitioner are where no injury has occurred, but the court is required to resolve issues of fault and/or the quantum (value) of losses. I still do these cases occasionally now, but I am increasingly instructed in fast-track and multi-track cases.

NB: *What is multi-track work?*

RTC: There are three case management tracks in civil claims: the small claims track, the fast track and the multi-track. The small claims track is for the lower value, more straightforward cases, the multi-track for higher value, higher complexity work and the fast track is for the cases in between. The fast track is the standard track for most low-value personal injury cases which would take a day to resolve at trial.

NB: *Isn't it a bit odd that work that where there's a higher value to the claim should get a different sort of procedure – because cases are all about the same issues aren't they?*

RTC: Not necessarily, the liability and quantum issues which arise in cases higher up the case management tracks are often far more complex and require far more evidence. In personal injury cases on the multi-track, there is often extensive medical evidence, complex issues of breach of duty and causation and various heads of losses claimed. For instance, if someone suffered a catastrophic injury in a road traffic accident, the claim is likely to include damages for personal injury as well as for the provision of losses including medical treatment, care and lost earnings. Therefore, while similar liability issues may arise in a small claim road traffic case, the multi-track case will be far more complex.

The legal and evidential issues arising in higher value claims can be technical, the evidence is generally more extensive and the issues may require a greater degree of scrutiny and assessment. Multi-track cases involve more case management hearings, more preparation and costs are higher. A lot of personal injury cases allocated to the fast track have fixed costs imposed so there may be less scope for counsel's involvement in case preparation before trial.

NB: *Do you do a bit more multi-track now than you did at the start?*

RTC: Yes, I do a lot more than I did at the start. Multi-track and fast-track work takes time to build up. It is also more likely that you will be instructed on a discreet piece of work rather than as retained counsel for the entire proceedings, especially at the start of your practice. In my experience, the paperwork starts before court work in the higher value, higher complexity cases. As a junior civil practitioner, your first experience of multi-track work may be drafting a set of particulars of claim or a schedule of loss. Then you may be instructed on an application hearing or a CCMC (Costs and Case Management Conference) hearing.

NB: *And for your professional development as you go forward then as a barrister in this type of work doing more multi-track cases is the right way to go clearly?*

RTC: Yes, definitely. The higher value and the higher complexity work is important. I would also say that diversification is important for practice development. For me, that means doing more clinical negligence, civil liberties and more inquest work.

NB: *Clinical negligence, that's where people have suffered injuries isn't it?*

RTC: Yes, it is where people suffer personal injury potentially as a result of medical negligence. This may be a specific injury which is caused by a negligent act, for instance, where an error is made during surgery.

Alternatively, it may be where an illness or disease has developed as a consequence of a failure to diagnose or treat a patient. Some cases also involve ethical issues related to consent. These cases invariably involve consideration of complex expert evidence from medical professionals. Some of the clinical negligence work which I do overlaps with inquest work, for instance where a death has arisen as a result of potentially negligent medical treatment or care.

NB: *Do you then go on to act in clinical negligence proceedings for the people that you've acted for the inquests?*

RTC: Yes, that is generally how the proceedings interrelate. A solicitor may act for the family of a deceased person in a civil claim and may also provide representation for the inquest. It can be hard to get funding for the inquest, sometimes families will be unrepresented at an inquest but have legal representation for a civil claim.

NB: *Have you done inquest work that is outside the field of clinical negligence?*

RTC: Yes, although most of my inquest practice to date has been in the clinical negligence field. I have acted in other inquests including road traffic collisions, cases where the cause of death was unknown and mental health deaths.

NB: *So looking at the spread of your work there's the more multi-track type of personal injury cases and related cases, there's the inquest work and clinical negligence anything else?*

RTC: Yes, I have a background in police law and worked for the independent Police Complaints Commission (now the Independent Office for Police Conduct) prior to coming to the Bar. Building on this, my practice also includes actions against the police and other public bodies. This includes cases where people have been falsely imprisoned, suffered an unlawful arrest or have been discriminated against. It also can include claims under the Human Rights Act 1998. I act for individuals in claims against the state and I have also acted for public bodies including the police. I am also developing a Court of Protection practice.

NB: *And if we rewind to Rebecca Titus-Cobb at Bar School, if I'd asked you then to imagine what work you would be doing now, what do you think you would have said?*

RTC: I definitely would have anticipated that I would have a civil practice in light of my interests and career aims. The starting point for me would have been civil work rather than family or crime. At Bar School and when looking for pupillage, most students are faced with those three general paths or a common law pupillage (though of course there are exceptions to this). I was also offered pupillage during Bar School so I did know what my pupillage would be in and had a general idea of the types of cases which I may do as a junior practitioner. However, I do not think it is until you start pupillage that you fully appreciate how the first few years of practice may look in reality – it is a steep learning curve!

NB: *If you have in your mind those sorts of cases that you've got ongoing right now, what sort of tasks have you had to do involving the skills taught at Bar School for example advice, drafting or advocacy?*

RTC: The core vocational modules: conference, advocacy, drafting and advice build foundational skills which I draw upon on a daily basis. For example, one of my recent cases is an appeal against the decision of the Criminal Injuries Compensation Authority (CICA). My client was the victim of a serious assault with a weapon and suffered severe physical and psychological injuries. He is appealing the determination of the compensation awarded to him under the CICA scheme. I have held a conference with him in order to explore his evidence and take his instructions. In that conference, I provided verbal advice as to the merits of his appeal, the prospective grounds of appeal and the future procedural steps. I drafted the grounds of appeal and I will represent him at the oral hearing before the first tier tribunal. In another case, a recent inquest, I cross examined a forensic pathologist and then drafted written submissions on the conclusions available to the coroner.

NB: *Is the appeal to a court or tribunal?*

RTC: It is to the first tier tribunal.

NB: *And if you think about the sort of people or organisations who have mainly been your clients occasionally, it's the police authority or it could be the individual, but in other cases do you act for the hospital trust in negligence cases as well as for people who are making the claim?*

RTC: I represent both claimants and defendants, it is fairly mixed, but I probably do more claimant work, especially in the higher value cases. For defendants, I often act on behalf of insurers and I have also acted for the police and hospital trusts. The majority of my clinical negligence work is claimant work, it is more difficult to get instructions from defendants earlier in your practice. I mostly represent bereaved families at inquests.

NB: *What percentage of your work time is spent in court or tribunals versus working at your desk?*

RTC: I would say probably 50/50 under usual circumstances when I was attending court regularly. More hearings are now remote so it is far more time spent at my desk and less time at court or travelling.

NB: *If you think about the courts and tribunals that you attend, we talked inquests which are relatively informal, investigative, hearings before the coroner, and we talked about being in the County Court and occasionally the criminal injuries tribunal. Are there any other types of court or tribunal that you appear before?*

RTC: I have been instructed a few times to attend the Crown Court for a noting brief. These have all been related to driving offences, namely death by dangerous driving. I attended on behalf of an insurer, either the insurer of the deceased or one of the drivers. In those circumstances, the insurer requests a complete note of the criminal proceedings as this may inform any future civil claim. The Court of Protection is a distinct court.

NB: *The Crown Court work obviously is a wig and gown job; do you wear your wig and gown for any other type of occasions?*

RTC: Very occasionally you can do as a civil practitioner. Any fast-track or multi-track trial that you attend can be robed so it usually involves you having to take your robes to court and keep them in your bag or in the Advocates' Room. It is at the judge's discretion whether or not they robe, they rarely do.

NB: *What parts of your practice you find the most interesting? Are there are any areas that some people might find less exciting?*

RTC: I enjoy legal research and the advisory elements of my practice. My strengths lie in the analytical skills needed to practice at the Bar. I enjoy legal analysis and considering the complex issues in a case, for instance, researching and preparing an Advice or a skeleton argument. For those who thrive on the drama and thrill of advocacy in front of a jury, the prospect of sitting down with case law to read and a complex Advice to prepare may not be as exciting.

The clinical negligence and inquest work which I do can be fairly complex and technical, especially on issues of causation, I find this aspect of my practice both intellectually challenging and fulfilling. Getting to the crux of a clinical negligence case and working out the strengths or weaknesses in the claim will often involve sitting down with an expert clinician (usually a consultant) in conference and drilling down into complex issues of medical and legal causation. Similarly, in inquests, the witnesses giving evidence in court will often be expert witnesses such as pathologists or clinicians involved in the deceased's care (in the case of medical deaths). This requires a forensic style of cross-examination which I enjoy.

NB: *Of course a main question for the coroners courts is how the deceased died. I totally understand the causation interest to a civil lawyer.*

RTC: Yes, that's the primary question which the coroner is interested in. In inquests where Article 2 of the European Convention on Human Rights is engaged, the scope is wider and the coroner will consider the circumstances surrounding the death. This usually arises where there has been contact with state agencies before death.

NB: *Have you been led yet?*

RTC: Not yet, that is something I would like to do.

NB: *Can I ask about the extent to which your time in practice has so far matched or differed from expectations when you are doing the Bar course? Students may not always know what to expect in that change from studying law even at a practical level at Bar School to actually practising it. I wondered whether you thought Bar School prepared you for what your practice has become and is becoming?*

RTC: At Bar School you probably do not anticipate that the skill set which you will utilise on a day-to-day basis, and the type of tasks that you will undertake depends on the type of practice that you have. For me, I knew that my strengths lay in my analytical skills and written advocacy, so I wanted to develop a paperwork practice as well as a court practice. That was one of the attractions of civil law because, rather than being primarily an advocate in court, I also have the opportunity to do written advocacy and there is a lot of legal analysis involved.

Bar School does prepare you for that to an extent, but I think that understanding can only come from seeing the work that barristers in different practice areas do. It is important to consider your own skill set, what are your strengths and weaknesses, and therefore, what type of work may be better suited to you. There is perhaps a tendency as a student or when seeking pupillage to focus only on the areas of law which interest you, rather than considering the kind of work which you will do day to day and whether that will suit your skill set.

NB: *They are all really good points Rebecca, it's a really good way putting it. I suppose Bar School aims to get you at least to the required minimum standard in all the different skills that it is anticipated barristers will need. But when you actually start practising, it's up to you, isn't it, as the individual, to make sure that you exploit the skills you've learned and make yourself better?*

RTC: Exactly. I think it's about recognising where your interests lie but also what your strengths are. Some people will naturally be more suited to family work because they have the required skill set for that type of work, others may be better placed to practise in commercial law for the same reason.

NB: *Were there any subject areas at university or Bar School that you took and, when your practice began, you were glad that you had taken?*

RTC: I think the core vocational modules at Bar School are vital to developing the skills which you use on a daily basis. For instance, you need to have a broad understanding of how to draft pleadings or structure an Advice, an appreciation of cross-examination techniques and how to structure oral submissions. The conference module is also an invaluable one. You can quite easily fall into a trap of just treating a conference as a conversation with a client, solicitor or an expert. However, the emphasis which the course module places on structure and preparation is key to a successful conference. I still go through the same process which I was taught at Bar School when preparing for a conference or drafting an agenda. There have been times when I've not gone through that process and it has not been as effective.

NB: *As you made that change from Bar School I suppose through pupillage and into tenancy was there any particular change that you have to get used to that was more difficult?*

RTC: Probably being in charge of your own time and managing your own workload. The workload is heavy and you will inevitably work long hours including some weekends. However, it can be manageable provided you are strict and work efficiently. In pupillage, there is generally an expectation that you are in Chambers during normal working hours so, while you will work in the evenings, there should be enough time to get the work done. As a tenant, provided you maintain your professional obligations to attend hearings and conferences, the rest of your time is yours to work as you wish. This can make it quite difficult to draw boundaries between work and non-work time and I think it is important to be strict about when you work and when you switch off. I tend to work later in the day and also I work better under pressure so there can be a temptation to take the afternoon off if you finish early or have the morning off on a quiet day. Obviously, flexibility is a huge benefit to the job and if you can, take that time off, just ensure that you will not pay for it later!

NB: *One of the last areas and I'm coming to you now is about your developing work life and work-life balance, and it's suppose first, I wondered when you're not in court do you tend to work in Chambers or at home? I'm getting the impression from you that it's at home mostly – but it's tricky because we've been in coronavirus times?*

RTC: Yes, the past few months have been unusual to put it mildly. I think I've been to court three or four times in the past in the past few months. During pupillage and in my first year of tenancy, I lived in Manchester city centre very close to Chambers so I spent much more time in Chambers. During pupillage, I was in Chambers every day. After tenancy, you can make those decisions yourself. I still did like to base myself in Chambers quite a lot, if my work was I local to Chambers I would probably go in after court. Under normal circumstances, I probably work from home at least one day a week and generally go into Chambers two or three times a week.

NB: *Do you work in the evenings?*

RTC: Yes.

NB: *In Chambers do you have your own room; is it all about hot desking?*

RTC: During pupillage, I shared my supervisor's room and then when I got tenancy I moved to a room with other junior tenants and one of my co-pupils. We also have a library at Chambers and generally a lot of the junior tenants will congregate there. I usually work a lot from the library because it is a good social space.

NB: *How techy or your practice areas? Is it is a job wholly less paper-based now more digital or not?*

RTC: As a Chambers, we are fairly progressive and technology driven so we are very much encouraged to utilise the IT services which we have available to us. All case files are contained online and that is how I access my papers for cases. I very rarely get paper files.

NB: *What about in the courts and tribunals, are they very techy?*

RTC: It varies and seems to have changed a lot in light of the Covid-19 pandemic with more hearings now taking place remotely. In some regional courts, you may struggle to get a plug, but in others, particularly the main court centres, there are better facilities. Courts are increasingly utilising video platforms, which, while there are undoubtedly problems at times, is a step in the right direction. More electronic bundles are also used in court hearings.

I was conscious at the start of my practice that I did not want to be too reliant on paper so I have developed working practices which are more tech-friendly, for instance preparing a bookmarked and annotated bundle which can be used as a live working document. I generally use a PDF on my iPad as my bundle in court.

NB: *Would you describe practising in your fields of law to be sociable, collegiate or is a lot of time spent by yourself?*

RTC: I think it is what you make of it. In civil there is probably not as much time spent in court as in other practice areas. For instance, colleagues who are family or criminal practitioners will spend a lot of the time at the same courts, and for longer cases, I think that helps build a collegiate atmosphere. In my practice, I probably travel more so that means I spend more time by myself.

NB: *Travel is one of the things I wanted to ask about, too?*

RTC: I am mostly based in the North West but I can travel across the country. My Chambers have sites in Manchester, Chester, Liverpool and Sheffield, so the work which I get tends to be anywhere across the northern half of England or Wales. My practice is more concentrated in the North West because I practise from the Manchester Chambers and I am clerked from Manchester but I also have been further afield than that. This year, I have been to Ipswich, London and Cumbria. I travel a lot.

NB: *Did you expect that?*

RTC: I probably didn't realise how much travel was involved. I think some working practices have changed since the pandemic and will probably not revert back. Some of the hearings which are now happening remotely are unlikely to go back to being in person. I anticipate going forward that I will travel less than I did previously, and incoming pupils and junior barristers may not travel as much as I did in the first few years of practice.

NB: *What are typical hours of work – if there is a typical?*

RTC: I tend to work later in the day as I am more of a night owl than an early bird. Under normal circumstances, my typical hours of work would usually involve me leaving home to travel to court at around 7.30am or 8am to get to court for 9:00/9:30. I would probably be in court for a few hours or to the early afternoon but that does vary case to case. I would then either go to Chambers for a few hours or back home. I generally have a few hours off late afternoon or early evening and then possibly work from say 8pm to midnight to prepare for the following day.

NB: *Wellbeing is an important focus of the Bar Council now, but it wasn't always. When I was called to the Bar in 1994, wellbeing wasn't on anybody's radar at all. How do you find the work-life balance in your fields of law?*

RTC: One misconception which I had at Bar School and even at the start of pupillage was that I would not be able to ask for time off or that there would be an expectation on me to work all hours of the day, seven days a week. While the expectations do vary from Chambers to Chambers, my experience has been very positive. I have no issue with asking for time off or for preparation or paperwork days. In fact, that is encouraged in my Chambers. There has been a couple of times where I've felt overwhelmed or where I was working beyond the limits of my capacity, but I had help from my clerks to navigate through those busier times. I hope that is the situation at other Chambers as well. There appears to be a cultural change underway at the Bar which recognises that the work-life balance needs to be better, and there is a big focus on promoting wellbeing. However, you do have to actively manage this yourself, it is important to check in with yourself, look at how busy you are and whether you are coping. It can be easy to keep going at a fast pace and not recognise when you are overstretched or overburdened.

NB: *It is having that self-awareness isn't it, which can be difficult sometimes?*

RTC: I would say in my experience that I work best when I'm busy and I like to work under pressure. The reality of my practice is that I am busy and I do work a lot, however, it is important to recognise when it gets too much. In this job there is a tendency to keep pushing forward, so it's important to be self-aware.

NB: *Diversity, we are keen to know about experiences of sex equality, race equality, social mobility, other areas that you consider touch* *on the issue of diversity at the Bar. Do you have any experience or observations?*

RTC: This is a hugely important issue and one which many barristers, myself included, are extremely passionate about. It is important that the Bar represents a diverse cross-section of society and that no person, irrespective of background, feels excluded from a career at the Bar.

Gratefully, there seems to be increased awareness and attention being given to the issue of diversity at the Bar, but of course much more still needs to be done. There are a number of new initiatives which have been recently set up to encourage access to the Bar, including Bridging the Bar, which my Chambers is involved in. The Bar Council have done a lot of active campaigning including the 'I am the Bar' campaign.

I come from a state school background and am the first lawyer in my family. The Bar was a complete unknown to me, and I think it is important that those who have an interest are able to experience and understand what the life entails. Initiatives like Bridging the Bar are crucial to this. One element that has helped me personally was the availability of funding through the Inns of Court and at Bar School. I would have struggled to put myself through Bar School without this, such matters are invaluable to increasing social mobility and access to the Bar.

Unfortunately, many barristers still experience overt and latent types of discrimination at the Bar I think we have to be realistic that that does exist. We all need to do what we can to address the underlying issues and challenge discrimination and unconscious bias.

NB: *Is there something that you can say about income progression in the early years of practice?*

RTC: In my experience, income progresses quite quickly with a civil practice. I was very concerned at the start of pupillage that I wouldn't be paid because I was told things can get tied up with insurers and it can be slow. That wasn't really my experience, I have always had enough to get by. However, income does vary month to month and that is something to be to be aware of particularly at the start of your career where you are probably living month to month and maybe you haven't had the time to build up savings. My advice to junior practitioners would be don't get too excited if you have a really great month because in all likelihood, the next month might not be the same.

NB: *The last thing is just about the future, if you have any thoughts about the future of the Bar in the areas that you work in or generally?*

RTC: In the area that I work in there is a lot of change on the horizon and this is likely to disproportionately impact upon the junior bar. In particular, there are incoming changes to the costs regimes for low-level personal injury work and there may be less 'bread and butter' type work available. Any barrister going into civil law needs to be aware of and plan for those changes. In my practice group, we have all been discussing how we overcome the issues and what type of work we need to be looking at to fill the gaps. I think there is a need to recognise the issues and be prepared to diversify. This means being creative and looking at other practice areas that may complement the more traditional areas of personal injury work.

4 Property, Planning, Public Law

An Interview with Joel Semakula, Landmark Chambers

NB: *Joel, tell me when you began your tenancy?*

JS: In 2020. I have been a tenant for almost a year.

NB: *Which areas of law have you practised in since you began your tenancy?*

JS: It is quite varied. I do all of Chambers' main areas which are property, planning and public law. I have a commercial background so do some commercial law. My work in environmental law mostly comes under the planning umbrella. I often do pro bono work for the Environmental Law Foundation, where they approach Chambers for an Advice in relation to a potential planning law challenge on environmental grounds. Once I produce that Advice, if it's meritorious, then I will continue to work on the actual claim.

They are a fantastic organisation and I have already had success with one judicial review claim to limit activity on a motocross site partly on environmental law grounds. That was my first solo judicial review and I am glad it went well. That is one example of the kind of environmental law work we do.

There have also been a number of other times where I have produced an Advice in the environmental law space where I have to tell the client there is really nothing we can do. I have to say that we just do not have the statutory regime or the common law support that I think you were expecting. It is difficult to use the law to enforce environmental standards against individuals. In those circumstances, the answer is often that you have to look for different tools that may help you to achieve the same or similar goals.

With big changes such as the pending Environmental Law Bill, I am excited about the opportunities in this area of law and do think the

DOI: 10.4324/9781003111597-5

future is bright for people who seek to use the law to protect the environment and enforce their rights. I am excited to see how that develops, am hoping to write more and become a leader in this field.

NB: *What has become clear to me with my interviews is that it is difficult to summarise in two or three words what a barrister's practice area is these days.*

JS: I think it depends on the set. The juniors at some Chambers very clearly do one area of work, e.g. property. I happen to be at a set that is really committed to having broader areas of work, and at the junior end most of us do everything. Some people have come in probably within a year or two drop one of our key three areas, but I really enjoy all of them and see myself trying to stick with as many of them for as long as I can. I imagine if you ask me this question four years from now, I may only have two left!

NB: *Are these the sort of practice areas where you wanted to work, or has it changed as you have gone through your legal training?*

JS: I think as a student barrister initially I was quite committed to a commercial practice and that was partly driven by having enjoyed contract law at university and partly by my understanding of it coming from a background in finance. As I began exploring the profession and exploring different sets, I was also drawn to Chambers that did property work. This was why I ended up applying to Landmark for their specialist property pupillage and also to other property sets. I was attracted to the opportunity at Landmark to do property work, in addition to the chance to explore public law, which was an area that I had always been interested in.

The other big thing is planning, which I probably spend about a third of my practice doing. However, very few students know what a planning practice is like and do not have much exposure to it either at law school or at Bar School or even in mini pupillages. I would say that planning is an area that I truly discovered during pupillage and is now an area that I really enjoy. I think it is going to be part of my practice for a very long time. I particularly love the opportunity to do environmental work that flows from a planning practice.

NB: *How would you describe the split in those areas that you have described?*

JS: I would say I am about 40% property, 40% planning and about 20% public.

NB: *Can you give me some examples of the types of cases that you are instructed in right now?*

JS: On the public law side of things, I have been instructed for about eight months now by NHS Blood & Transplant Service, which is one of the core participants in the ongoing Infected Blood Inquiry. That will be on for potentially another year and takes about one day a week out of my practice.

On the property side, I am in the process of writing an Advice in a co-ownership dispute between a mother and daughter. I am advising the daughter. The pair bought property together, however, the relationship has subsequently broken down and the question is who owns what percentage of the property. Many of us will remember this from law school where the parties are often husband and wife and following the breakdown of the relationship, there are many cases about what share of the property the wife gets. I have also spent a lot of last week, this week and likely next week doing possession cases.

So I usually spend about two days a week acting for landlords in these hearings as they seek to secure possession of, mainly, residential properties.

I also recently completed my first planning inquiry where I was acting for a residents group that was resisting a development for the building of 30 homes including 26 affordable homes on green belt land. So that is the kind of a mix of what has been keeping me busy.

NB: *Is the Infected Blood Inquiry, or IBI, a statutory inquiry?*

JS: Yes, it is. Much like the well-known Grenfell Inquiry launched in response to that tragedy. The IBI came from a scandal in the 1970s and 1980s in which many people were transfused with contaminated blood which led to them being infected with diseases such as HIV and Hepatitis C. There has been a huge campaign to properly investigate what happened with the hope of ensuring it never happens again. I am acting for the Blood Service as part of a big team of solicitors and barristers and being led by Charlie Cory-Wright at 39 Essex.

NB: *You have already talked about writing Advices as a regular feature of your work. What about other things that more students will be studying? My students this year are just starting on their induction week today, they will study drafting and advocacy; do you engage in those activities regularly?*

JS: If I have a think about the three of four tasks that I do most regularly as a junior barrister – they are drafting pleadings, writing Advices and preparing for the advocacy involved in short hearings. Possession hearings for example take 15 or 20 minutes in the courtroom but the prep time can be much longer than that. The one I am attending tomorrow probably took me four hours today to prepare. The final thing is I would say is that Advice means usually advising in writing and advising in conference. There are some other smaller tasks that make up part of what I do including writing pre-action letters and reviewing submissions for approval.

I have also done a couple of investigations where I have been instructed by a local authority, which has received a corporate complaint from a member of the public. I act as the independent investigator for them on such complaints where there is a planning issue.

I had a conversation with my clerk some time back where I said I want more cross-examination experience. I would say, in the second six months of my first year, I have actually had the chance to do a lot more of it. I think cross-examination is a very different skill to everything else we really do as barristers, and it takes years to become truly excellent at it.

NB: *What sort of cases or hearings have led you to be cross-examining?*

JS: The most recent one was my planning inquiry which involved cross-examining two planning experts. It was a little bit of a nerve-wracking experience to begin with but examining an expert really tests your skills. I'm glad I got to gain some experience in doing this within my first year of practice! I have also cross-examined in fast-track trials, in property damage trials and in service charge trials.

There is rarely any cross-examination in possession proceedings. It usually just involves consideration of an application for an order. The landlord has to satisfy the judge that he has fulfilled all the criteria in order to be entitled to that order.

NB: *If we look at the sorts of people or organisations who have typically been your clients next; we have already talked about the Infected Blood Inquiry. You mentioned also in possession hearings, you are acting mainly for landlords?*

JS: Yes, I mainly act for landlords. I have acted a few times on a pro bono basis for defendant tenants, where I have taken instructions from the pro bono charity *Advocate*. In the planning world, I often act for local authorities, individuals or residents' groups. At my level, it is less likely that I will act for a developer on my own without being led.

NB: *What has your case load been compared with your second six months' pupillage?*

JS: It's funny because unlike my colleagues at the criminal bar, I did not have a fully practising second six. What I mean by that is that my criminal barrister friends began to take on a pretty full caseload of their own from the outset. Whereas in my areas of work, I was taking on fewer cases and still being closely supervised. My caseload in practice now is significantly greater because I was not actually on my feet very much in my second six and that is just the nature of pupillage at Landmark.

NB: *What percentage of your time would you say you have been spending in court or other tribunal-type settings compared with working at your desk, and which courts and tribunals do you attend?*

JS: I would say approximately two days a week and I am happy with that. Much of the bread-and-butter work of most junior civil lawyers takes place in the County Courts. You never know what you are going to get in that setting. In terms of other tribunals/courts, I would say that over the last three months, I have been in the High Court, appeared before an inspector in a planning inquiry and before a disciplinary committee of a local council. So those are probably the four very different types of tribunals have made up my most recent practice. What I would say is, only once have I had to wear the wig and gown and that was when I was in the High Court. I do not actually own one yet. The rest of the time I am just in my regular suit.

NB: *What parts of your practice would you say you find the most interesting and what areas do some people maybe find less exciting?*

JS: My favourite part of this job is the advocacy. What I particularly like about the property and planning work I have been doing is the amount of advocacy experience I am getting. The reality is the public law work that I do is the stuff that is much more likely to end up in the news so things like assisting in the *Shamima Begum* case or working on the Covid 'A' levels results scandal. That kind of public interest work is unlikely to have me doing the advocacy before a judge (I'm just too junior) but it's probably the sort of work that people are much more likely to hear about in the media. That has a different kind of appeal and those cases are very interesting as well.

What do people find less exciting? Some people find too much written work probably a little bit less exciting. In the context of being a pupil in Covid, and then a first-year tenant in Covid, there wasn't much court work and so nobody was really getting into court. I did a lot of paperwork in my second six and also probably a lot more than I do now in the first half of my year in tenancy. Now we are seeing the courts beginning to work through their backlogs and I am in court all the time. I like a nice mix, but I think if my practice were 100% paperwork or 100% sitting behind somebody in court, that would be quite a different job that what I thought I had signed up for.

NB: *It's the variety, isn't it? That is what I like about the Bar – going to different places, seeing different people, and it's different sorts of things that you do.*

JS: The unpredictability! On the one hand, it's great; on the other hand, sometimes it is not your best friend!

NB: *You have talked about being led already but just wondering what sort of tasks did being led involve you doing?*

JS: I have been led a few times. I can think of two cases that have been the most substantive. One of them was a planning judicial review where we were acting for the claimant. I did the first draft of the claim which was quite substantial. The hope was we were going to get to file that in court but unfortunately (although fortunate for my client), the local authority settled and so the case was resolved by a consent order.

I had a much more longer-term opportunity of being led where I was working on an examination in proceedings for a development consent order. Historically, when you had a large infrastructure project, the developer would need to get planning permission in each local authority through which the project passed. In order to avoid that and in light of how long it took to get permission for the fifth terminal at Heathrow, the government introduced development consent orders. So now the process is akin to a big planning inquiry that allows the developer to get all of the required permissions via this one process. These are pretty big projects.

I was actually led by my former supervisor, Richard Turney, and we were acting for the highways authority and local transport authority in the Development Consent Order (DCO) process for the AQUIND Interconnector Project, which is a new subsea and underground high-voltage direct current electric power transmission link between the south coast of England and Normandy in France.

NB: *What did you do in that DCO?*

JS: The biggest things we did there were advising the client on the appropriate response to specific parts of drafting in the DCO and giving legal advice on highways and compulsory acquisition issues. I also deputised for my leader when he was not able to attend the actual examination and made submissions before the Examining Authority. That was a first and I enjoyed it. I am hoping to be led a bit more over the next year. I think it is a tough mix. I love my solo practice – I love the control that you get of running your own cases – but I am a big believer that being led is such a key part to your development as a junior barrister.

NB: *I agree because at the very least, you get to be involved in cases that are more immense than ones you might be instructed in, in your own right.*

JS: Yes. Also, it is tough to get feedback in this job because we spend so much time working by ourselves. Often the only feedback you get is not being instructed again. The type of feedback that would be most useful would be somebody showing you if there is a better way to do something. So just working closely with somebody who has been in this game a little bit longer than you means that you get that feedback. In my view, one year into a job it is really important to still be learning in that way. I expect that will remain the case for a long time.

NB: *I think it is the worst barristers who never think that way. They think that their way is the only way, and they never advance in terms of their personal presentation or abilities. Can you tell me whether your time in practice so far has matched or been different from expectations that you had when you were back on the Bar course. Did Bar School prepare you for what your practice is now becoming?*

JS: I am not sure Bar School could have prepared me for the amount of remote hearings I have done this early into my practice. Nobody knew what that was going to be like. Let us take the example of cross-examination. It is tough to compare the way we were taught to do it at Bar School with how you do it over a computer where you have got your client WhatsApping you on one screen, you are trying to take a note of the cross-examination for your closing speech on another screen while listening to the answer that you are receiving, thinking about the next question that you need to ask and then trying to make sure you get everything that you need for your closing speech!

You just have a lot more going on than you did in Bar School. At the same time, you have a number of cases you are taking on, and it's surprising how quickly you have to shift focus. You start working on something at 9am, but by 10am you are getting phone calls about one of your other cases. There are those constant shifts. I am not sure how Bar School can prepare you for that. That's one of the things that is so different about life in practice from pupillage and from Bar School.

I think the thing that Bar School prepares you quite well for are things like client management and understanding what the ethics are, even though I think what you experience in practice can often be quite difficult to predict. Often if you are very junior, you are against litigants in person and we are constantly asking ourselves, do I need to inform the court of this potential argument against me, or do I need to raise that particular issue?

NB: *Were there any subject areas that you studied at university or at Bar School which, when you were starting out in your practice, you thought, I am glad I took that because that's really helped me?*

JS: Yes, I studied judicial review which was great. I am glad I did judicial review because just procedurally, it's very different studying administrative law whilst learning practically how to prepare and argue a judicial review claim. It's just so important to what I do now.

NB: *What are the most difficult changes that you have got used to as you have settled into your practice?*

JS: I would say the first thing is, and I have spoken about this on Twitter a little bit, that it is rare that whatever I think I am going to achieve when I start work at 9am on a Monday is achieved by 5pm that day. This is just because of the number of cases you run as a very junior person at the Bar. It is a reflection of the unpredictability of what could happen on something that you are already instructed on. That can often be a difficult change.

Also diary management can be quite tough. There are a lot of moving parts to managing your diary: from understanding when you do actually have room to take on another case to staying on top of the number of people that have demands on your time. There is the perpetual challenge of things taking much longer than you quoted because you are seeing them for the first time. All of that comes into managing your diary and obviously you get assistance with that at the Bar and from your clerks, but for me that is still a big learning point. Sometimes, it does not go well. Miracles happen: a case falls out sometimes and you think, I'm glad that has gone because I do not know how this was all going to get done.

NB: *When you are working on your papers, do you tend to do it at home or in Chambers?*

JS: I am probably at home two days a week and then three days a week in Chambers. Ideally for me as someone starting out, I want to be in Chambers three to four days a week.

NB: *Do you have your own room in Chambers?*

JS: No, I share with a colleague who also does property law who is about five years senior to me and that is fantastic. It is great to have her as a roommate especially in my first year. I would highly recommend that to everyone.

NB: *How techy are your practice areas leading into issues about whether the job is more paper-based or more digital? Is it ring binders or is it hard drives?*

JS: I made a decision quite early on as a pupil that I was going to make myself a techy barrister so I do everything I can to be paperless. It doesn't always work for two reasons – sometimes I get sent documents via email in a disorganised way that means it is not very efficient or easy for me to work on a screen. In those circumstances, I have to print things off.

The other thing I have found since we have gone back to court is that judges are not always as techy as you might want them to, and what I mean by that is that it is often the system to blame. You can't always be sure that if your instructing solicitors send the bundle to the court, it will be there when you arrive. You take a big risk not arriving with a printed bundle! It seems to me it does slightly defeat the purpose of being paperless if I still have to print a bundle and give it to the judge. Right now, that is something for me that is truly holding us back as a profession. I would rather just show up to the court with my laptop and an iPad. At the moment, I am perfectly happy to be 100% paperless but for all these reasons, I am finding it a bit more of a challenge.

NB: *Are the fields of law that you work in sociable and collegiate or is it very solitary?*

JS: It is a good question. I would say Chambers is very sociable and collegiate. When you are working in all of these areas, you tend to be working on your own unless you are being led. So, I think there is a lot of time spent working alone at a desk. The way that you get around that is by being in Chambers, sharing a room, that kind of stuff. I am a big extrovert and not very good in my own company. This is why the solitary nature of our job continues to be something that I find challenging. This was of course much worse during pupillage at the start of the pandemic.

NB: *What are your typical hours of work? How are you able to organise it?*

JS: I tend to start around 8.45am and I try and get off around 6.30pm/7pm. I avoid most weekends, it's usually the odd one.

NB: *Is there a lot of travelling for you?*

JS: I was a remote barrister for a lot of my first year in practice but over the last three months, if I am in court, I am probably travelling about two days a week. So yesterday, I was in Slough, today I was in Uxbridge. Tomorrow, I think I am in Central London.

NB: *So, everything within reach as it were?*

JS: To an extent. I had a case in Sleaford and another one in Birmingham, the day before that. Every day, I look at my diary and think where am I going tomorrow?

NB: *Did you have any expectations about the travelling before you started at the Bar or did you always know?*

JS: I always understood that life as a junior civil barrister is spent traversing the County Courts of England and Wales. I expected that, but then Covid hit and I spent all of my time doing all my hearings remotely so it didn't matter where the court was based. Now, all of a sudden, I am moving around. I am slowly getting more and more used to it.

NB: *Tell me about wellbeing, because the Bar Council says that it is very big on wellbeing but certainly it never always was like that. When I was called in 1994, wellbeing was not even a word, I don't think. How is the work-life balance for you?*

JS: I used to be an investment banker so I know how bad it can get when it comes to lack of work-life balance. Probably that is why I think my work-life balance at the Bar is brilliant. I think part of that is led by our clerks. I happen to be in a set where the clerks are really good about helping you maintain some balance. They are really reasonable, and there is not a ton of pressure to absolutely kill yourself from the junior end. When you're practising, I think you have got to be aware of that. We all work very hard, but nobody looks at me like I'm crazy for leaving the office at 7pm. For me, that is pretty balanced.

I perform comedy on the side, and work doesn't really get in the way of that or my ability to spend time with people I love. Naturally, that's not true all the time because sometimes if I haven't managed my diary as effectively as I could, those hours do get worse. However, it hasn't happened enough for me that it's a problem.

I was on holiday over the summer and unfortunately partly because of an issue that arose on a case that I had already been instructed on, that did mean that I had to work for half of that holiday which is not ideal. I now understand a way to prevent something like that from happening again in the future. Generally, I think the work-life balance, at least in the areas that I do, is okay. I do not envy my colleagues at the criminal bar. I hear their stories of being in court five days a week, getting papers at half past five the night before. That kind of stuff doesn't really happen in my practice areas, which is key to maintaining that balance.

This also comes from, I have to say, a background where I used to do a job that involved getting to work at 10am, four days a week, and leaving for home between 1am and 4am in the morning. So, I am really against working in the evenings. I cannot stand it. I understand others do, but I did that for two years where I worked basically every weekend, 90 to 100 hours a week for two years. I am just not willing to live like that anymore.

NB: *Our next topic is diversity which is whether you have any experiences or observations about diversity in the Bar? We are keen to know all our interviewees' experiences of things like sex equality, race equality, social mobility in particular and any other areas that our interviewees consider touch on that broad topic of diversity at the Bar.*

JS: I tweeted yesterday about an experience that I had for the first time ever at the Bar. In all the years that I have been a mini pupil shadowing barristers and having spent a year as a judicial assistant at the Court of Appeal, yesterday was the first time that I have ever been in a courtroom where both the advocate and the judge are black men. I was the advocate. That was a unique experience and goes to the wider point of being a black man in civil law, particularly in areas like property, planning and commercial law. I am very used to being one of the few black men in the room, often the only one. That is my general experience of diversity in the areas of law in which I practise. I am vocal about how I think that needs to change. I spent a lot of time working with students and barristers particularly from these groups trying to see what we can do to change that.

In terms of social mobility, this is also an area that I am really interested in. It comes from own background. I am working class, state educated, grew up in an overcrowded council flat in the East End of London. I made it from there to these areas of the Bar. I think that is also really important. It is important also that the clients we work with, in particular in the property and public side of the work that I do, that people have experiences of all different types of barristers when they encounter the legal system. They potentially might encounter someone who has a better understanding of their background or their circumstances. I am clear that I think the Bar needs to do better on these issues. Personally, I am most interested in racial equality and social mobility.

I think things are getting better but I think it was telling that in all the time I have spent trying to become a barrister and then practising as one, yesterday was the first time I had ever had that kind of experience. It really impacted me.

NB: *What would you say is the sort of income progression in the areas that you work in?*

JS: Property and planning are higher paid areas of the Bar than public law. However, public law practitioners also do well in my Chambers. I always say to students that the best gauge you can get of what type or what you might expect your earnings to be like in your first year, is to look at the pupillage award. Generally, with the civil sets, first year tenants make more in that first year than whatever the pupillage award was, and my guess is that it is usually around 15% to 20% more.

In terms of progression, your income does climb quite quickly in the earlier years but it will plateau. Generally, if you get yourself in a good set with high-quality work, I think you can feel confident about good solid income progression. The three areas in which I practise most definitely have good progression.

NB: *What thoughts do you have about the future of the Bar in the areas where you work?*

JS: We can go back to diversity. The Bar, for years, has said it is embracing diversity and has a number of initiatives and programmes in place to really change the face of the Bar. This is about both recruitment and retention. I am very hopeful that the Bar is becoming a more diverse place and taking this issue seriously. My hope is that we are then going to see that really rising through the ranks of the profession. To me, success looks like greater diversity in those securing pupillage and tenancy, becoming silks and making it to the judiciary.

NB: *Are we succeeding with that?*

JS: The big issue is – regardless of all of these diversity and mentoring programmes – you are still seeing black candidates, even with the same grades as their white counterparts, failing to get pupillage at anywhere near the same rate.

There are other groups for which this is an issue, e.g. disabled candidates. The Bar really has got to take a look at this. None of this work matters if at the end of the day, diverse candidates do not get spots in Chambers. If they are not actually earning fees, doing cases, then all of these additional programmes really do just look like lip service. So my hope for the future is that we actually end up with tangible outcomes.

When it comes to the future for my practice, an area that is really interesting in the work we do at Landmark is environmental law. Personally, I am really excited to be at a Chambers that I think could lead the way as to how this area of practice develops. There are a lot of exciting things going on in this country with the new Environmental Bill, COP26 coming up and the new Office for Environmental Protection. I think this is a fantastic opportunity for junior practitioners and aspiring barristers to lead and also it is another way in which we as lawyers can make a difference.

Those are two quite different thoughts on the future but that is where I am.

5 Inquests, Public Law

An Interview with Ciara Bartlam, Garden Court North Chambers

NB: *When did your tenancy at Garden Court North begin, Ciara?*

CB: October 2019.

NB: *So at the date of our interview you have been in practice for about six months?*

CB: Six months and coronavirus!

NB: *Ha! Yes. What sort of work do you do, Ciara?*

CB: I would describe myself as a legal aid barrister and I do mainly civil work. Housing law is about 50% of my practice. The vast majority of housing work for a very junior tenant is suspending warrants of eviction which is the very last stage before somebody is evicted. Generally speaking, if you are a tenant, your landlord always has to go to court to evict you but this is your last-ditch attempt to stop it. What usually happens is you get the papers maybe the day before the hearing. You might have five or ten minutes with your client and then you go in and you try to persuade the judge to let them stay. The vast majority of cases are rent arrears cases, and usually my clients are people on benefits and specifically on Universal Credit. When they get to this very final stage, they usually have a suspended order for possession against them which says as long as you pay the rent and, say, £3.70 towards the arrears every week, you will not be evicted. When they see me at court it's generally because they have defaulted on that arrangement and usually the reason for the default is because of the way Universal Credit is paid, it's out of sync with their rent payments. Usually, in these circumstances, you're trying to persuade the court that they can afford the rent moving forward. There might be issues with their claim; there might be need for further information, usually it's just a matter of not having been paid to

DOI: 10.4324/9781003111597-6

date. So, you are doing whatever you can to persuade the judge who has an 'extended discretion'. It's very, very wide.

NB: *Did you say that was about 50% of your work?*

CB: Yes. It's about 50% of my work but not during coronavirus because there is a stay on possession proceedings so that is now zero percent of my work. The other areas that I do generally are all civil areas of practice that are publicly funded. I do immigration work. For example, one of the things that I have done quite regularly is bail applications. Where somebody is detained in immigration detention and they want to be released they can either apply to the Home Office or they can apply to the first tier tribunal. A tribunal is different from an ordinary court because it's more inquisitorial and less formal. In terms of bail, a lot of it is about how realistic it is that the Home Office is actually going to be able to deport them and it's also about how somebody's risk can be managed in the community, how likely are they to abscond, all of these sorts of things. So that's a large area of work for a junior barrister. I have also done lots of asylum claims, typically for Iraqi and Iranian Kurds.

The experience in the first tier tribunal is quite different from the County Court. In the County Court if I am doing housing, we might have a trial and of course everything is on the balance of probabilities. In the world of asylum, the standard of proof is actually much lower: it's 'a reasonable degree of likelihood'. The reason for that is if you are fleeing your country, you are unlikely to be able to collect easily all the records or evidence that you need to prove your claim. The dispute on the evidence usually boils down to the credibility of your client. It tends to be much more focused on legal arguments and on expert evidence and country evidence. So that's what I do in terms of immigration. I also do inquests, Court of Protection and welfare benefits because that ties in with everything, in my opinion.

NB: *Inquests, I take it, is mainly representing families at inquests?*

CB: Yes, so at Garden Court North, we do tend to take on publicly funded work and for that reason, we tend to represent bereaved families.

NB: *And you said Court of Protection, what is involved there?*

CB: Well, very junior work because the thing about the Court of Protection is that everybody who does it is usually pretty experienced. The sort of work that any junior barrister tends to do at the beginning of their practice is around deprivation of liberty, for example where somebody is in a care home and has a condition like dementia or Alzheimer's and expresses a wish to leave the care home, and that can be in any number of different forms, whether verbal or otherwise. It is for the court to determine in those circumstances whether, firstly, the person has capacity to make a decision themselves, because if somebody has the capacity and autonomy to make a decision themselves to leave, then they can just do that. Secondly, if the person is found to lack capacity to make that specific decision, the court has to determine whether it is in their best interests to be deprived of their liberty in that care home. This encompasses a consideration of whether it is really the least restrictive measure, because if you are depriving somebody of their liberty, of course, that is a huge intrusion on their rights and so it has to be the least restrictive way possible.

NB: *That's quite a range of work. Did you always want to do that sort of work or has it come as a surprise?*

CB: No, it's not really come as any surprise to me. I came to law by a sort of weird route. I actually have a housing background, but I read religion and theology at university and then I moved to Russia for three years. I came back and then I started working in housing, totally randomly. I worked as a homeless prevention officer for care leavers in particular, but 16- to 25-year-olds generally. That is actually where my interest comes from.

NB: *I wondered if you could just give me, maybe, two examples of the sorts of cases that you are instructed in right now?*

CB: One of the cases that I am instructed in is an inquest into the death of somebody who died in 2016/2017. It's been going on for a really long time, much longer than the 6 to 12 months' time that it should have taken. I am acting for a young adult whose mum very sadly died in 2017. There was some involvement from Children's Services at the time, and he knows that because he was a child at the time and he was aware of what was happening because he was, at that time, a teenager. Until now, the Coroner's Office hasn't actually got any information from Children's Services. It's been quite a long-standing process. There have been a lot of delays. Of course, it's very difficult for the family in those circumstances to get any amount of closure. We are now considering whether or not Article 2 is engaged. This is the right to life, and the reason that's important in inquest law is because it broadens the inquiry. Essentially, instead of the coroner looking at how someone died, they have to look at the circumstances in which the person died. This can change the conclusions that the court draws and can have quite a significant impact for the families.

Also, from a legal aid perspective, it's really important because at this stage, we do not have any funding. The majority of work that I've been doing on this case is pro bono (i.e. I won't get paid necessarily) because inquests are out of scope for legal aid. You need 'exceptional case funding' or ECF in order to obtain public funding for advocacy at hearings. You don't get that in all inquest cases and it's slightly easier to get it if the coroner rules that Article 2 is engaged, but it's by no means a certainty. There are some Article 2 inquests that don't ever get ECF.

NB: *Is it possible, for instance, that in any given inquest, you might do quite a lot of work and end up not being paid?*

CB: Yes. It's also the same for welfare benefits cases. It's the same for the majority of disrepair claims in housing. There are a number of significant areas that are out of scope for legal aid that people don't know about. So whilst I say that 50% of my practice is housing, it's also probably true to say that about 40% to 50% of my practice is also unpaid or at risk.

NB: *Some people might wonder why on earth you do it then?*

CB: I come from a background of privilege and I have been really fortunate in my life to have a family that really cares about me. It's not totally functional all the time but I have had an easy life. I have met people along the way in my life who haven't had that and it's not their fault. It's the system and the society that they are born into and for me, that seems like a really overwhelming injustice. I was always taught, when I was a child, to do whatever good you can with whatever skills you have, so for me it would be a waste if I didn't do this. There is no point in me being in law just to earn some money; that would be a waste of my skill. It would be a waste of my soul, to be honest.

NB: *Can I ask you about this. Twitter was alive in the summer about a Home Office tweet that seemed to point a finger of suspicion at what they called 'activist lawyers'. I don't quite know what it means but I know that it wasn't meant in a complimentary way. Would you describe yourself as an 'activist lawyer'?*

CB: I wouldn't necessarily describe myself as an 'activist lawyer' in the same way that I wouldn't describe myself as a female lawyer. I think you're either a lawyer or you're not. But I would certainly describe myself as somebody within the group of people who are usually called 'activist lawyers', if I can put it that way. To be honest, the thing is for legal aid lawyers and for anybody who is invested in trying to challenge the system and trying to get important outcomes for ordinary people, is that you are never going to be liked. It is like battering your head against a brick wall which is why I think that it is really important for young legal aid lawyers and barristers to know that there is an alliance of like-minded people around you. Somebody said in a webinar the other day that for her, the most important advice that you can ever give to somebody who is an aspiring lawyer is to find your tribe and that's a really vital part of sustaining yourself in this profession. I love it actually when they call us 'activist lawyers' because I know who those other people are who fall within that category.

NB: *I would like to ask you about your case load at the moment. My planned question is, what has your case load been like and how did it compare with your second six? But, of course, we have had coronavirus.*

CB: Before coronavirus I had cases that had stayed with me for a while. I had started to develop relationships with instructing solicitors and things were starting to go in a direction that was more interesting for me. I was doing crime in my second six but, whilst I would have loved to have done crime, I felt like a fish out of water. Now, with coronavirus, it's very different. As I said about the stay in possession proceedings, of course, I am not doing very much housing.

I am doing some injunction work which falls within housing, specifically anti-social behaviour injunctions. What we have found with the stay on possession proceedings is that landlords were trying all sorts of different ways to evict people by the back door. One of the ways you can do that is by getting an anti-social behaviour injunction against someone and then they breach it, which gives a mandatory ground of possession, or you get an anti-social behaviour injunction which includes a term that would exclude them from the property. As you can imagine, we have also seen an increase in homeless applications. There was some respite in that regard because we had an 'everyone in' instruction early on during the coronavirus pandemic from Luke Hall who is an MP. It meant that all rough sleepers would have to be accommodated. In principle, that should mean that there is no work to do in homelessness, but actually local authorities weren't accommodating people appropriately or into suitable accommodation.

In terms of the rest of my practice, I would say that during coronavirus my practice has been completely decimated. I don't have a full diary at all. I have been lucky to be in court maybe once or twice a week throughout which is not nearly as much as I would have been had it not happened. I have been very fortunate because I have been junior to a more senior member of Chambers in a welfare benefits case and that has earned me some money. Without that, I would be in dire straits to be honest. I am not entitled to the self-employed scheme because I became self-employed in 2018/2019.

NB: *What percentage of your time would you say you spend in courts or other tribunals and how much time working at your desk?*

CB: Pre-coronavirus, I think it would probably be about 50/50 but that is based on a seven-day week. I would be in court three or four times a week and then I would just be working all the way round.

NB: *You worked weekends a lot?*

CB: Yes I did, but I don't know if I necessarily needed to. My Chambers is really supportive so if I want a 'papers' day, I get a papers day. I think it's very difficult, particularly with me doing different areas of law, to feel competent in them without working a seven-day week, or a six-day week. I do take rest periods but there is so much to know, and it's not just about the substance of the law, it's also all the procedure and everything. Say, for example, you are representing a bereaved family at an inquest. I have got a case which is a natural causes death in custody. What that means is, where Article 2 would ordinarily be engaged because he is in the detention of the state, it's actually not in this case because there is no suggestion necessarily that the state contributed in any way to the death. But we still have the prison involved and the barrister that I'm against is 15 to 20 years' call and the only reason the family have me is because they have got no funding. If they had funding, they would have a much more experienced barrister but that's the reality of legal aid cuts. For a week-long inquest, I had to prep solidly for about a week.

NB: *A good example then of how a junior barrister can get very good experience, very quickly.*

CB: Exactly. It is, yes. But that's really a silver lining to a very dark cloud.

NB: *What sort of courts or other tribunals do you attend, and do you wear your wig and gown?*

CB: My wig doesn't even fit properly to be honest! In civil proceedings we do wear wigs and gowns for trials so, say, for example, if I do a disrepair trial in the County Court and we go to trial then I will wear my wig and gown. In tribunals you don't wear wigs and gowns ever. I don't know whether there is necessarily a written rule on that, but it just never happens.

NB: *What's a disrepair trial?*

CB: For me, it is usually for clients in social housing but it can be any tenancy. A landlord has obligations to keep in repair the structure and exterior of a property and when they don't do that, you can go to court. The problem is, again, this is out of scope for legal aid unless there is a risk to the health and safety of the occupant. The vast majority of social housing, it should be said, is in a state of disrepair, but the vast majority of tenants can't pursue it in court because there is no legal aid. That's where I step in. The trial is the 'trial of facts', so it's whether there exists disrepair, whether the landlord has been notified of it by the tenant, and whether they have had a reasonable period to complete the repairs and have failed to do so to a satisfactory standard. It's like any other trial, I suppose, in principle. I wear a wig and gown for committal proceedings, so when somebody has breached an injunction, because the court can commit them to prison and it's very serious. We do wear wigs and gowns for that and the standard, actually, in those proceedings is the criminal standard of proof.

NB: *Is it easy to say what part of your practice you find the most interesting and also at the other end of the scale, what areas some people may find less exciting?*

CB: I think people will find welfare benefits really not very exciting at all. The reason why I do it is because it's so important and because everybody should have, in my opinion, a subsistence level of benefit which is adequate to meet their daily living expenses. Unfortunately, as far as I see it, the state doesn't provide that currently and where people are sanctioned or refused benefits, all of that has to be challenged, in my view. The most interesting thing for me is inquest work – but I don't want that to sound like it detracts from the gravity of those proceedings for the families involved.

NB: *I don't think it takes anything away from the importance and gravity of the situation. It explains why lawyers get interested in areas of law. Often it's that drive, academically, that leads us on to explore those areas and helps us make such an important impact in the way that it's clear you do, Ciara.*

CB: Thanks, Nigel. Part of the reason why inquest law interests me is because it's an inquisitorial environment. I think you actually get closer to justice. Often justice is not just an outcome, it's a process. The thing about inquests that I like is the ability to engage with somebody on what is a very personal level, I think, and to guide them through a process which is otherwise really daunting. Of course, there's a lot at stake. We are talking about answers to a family's questions about how their loved one has died. We can be talking about closure. It's by no means easy but I feel like it's an area in which I have something to offer. I think that's why I enjoy it. It's raw, it really is. What you see in inquest work is all the ways in which all the consequences of state failure are thrown into very sharp focus, and out of that you have the ability to make significant change for many people. There is a wider impact of inquest work that I really love and that is often the most important thing for families as well: they will often say that the individual answers that they need are not necessarily the most important thing. The reason they pursue it so fearlessly and so graciously and so incredibly so much of the time is because they only hope that nobody else's family member ever suffers in the same way. I think that's the really incredible thing about inquests that makes it a special area of law.

NB: *Can I ask you about the case that you mentioned you are being led in at the moment by a senior member? What sort of work does that involve you doing in that role as junior counsel?*

CB: Anything he wants me to, basically! We have a couple of cases ongoing. One is about how many days there are in a year which sounds ridiculous, but the Secretary of State for Work and Pensions got it wrong, and we are now having an argument about that in court. What I have done in that case is drafting submissions and research. I also was responsible for all of the court bundles, liaising with the other side, liaising with solicitors and generally just doing all of the administrative tasks. My experience of it is maybe something different than what it's like usually because my senior is actually on paternity leave so that's part of the reason we have a second junior counsel because he is actually a junior counsel himself. So he's an incredibly supportive individual but he's not able to dedicate as much time to doing all the stuff around expert evidence, so that's kind of a lot of the stuff that I have been doing – contacting experts, working out what they might say on the issue and whether we need to have their evidence and then feeding that back.

NB: *When you talked about putting together bundles, what do you mean?*

CB: For a judicial review, the court will usually have a core bundle which has the letter of claim, the statement of facts and grounds, the response, all of those sorts of things. That will all be in there. It's my job then to put that all into a proper format, and during the coronavirus pandemic, all emphasis has been on bundles, so there are now certain ways that we have to do it. It has to be hyperlinked, the contents have to be bookmarked, so I do all of that. There is a core bundle and then there's the authorities bundle which is of course all the case law.

NB: *It's funny how time marches on because I remember when I was very junior barrister, even a law student in the holidays helping out places, putting together bundles meant you'd have a huge table and you would create piles of paper, about 15 or 20 bundles all the same!*

CB: Yes. IT skills are absolutely essential, and Adobe is my best friend. It's actually changed my life. I know that there are cheaper subscriptions out there but the fact is you can do everything you ever wanted to do with it. I actually get a little bit of joy out of bundles. It's like going to therapy, or gardening, it's got that therapeutic sort of quality to it. It's monotonous and mindless but at the end of it, you have something really beautiful!

NB: *Has your time in practice so far matched or differed from expectations that you had when you were on the Bar course?*

CB: I would say that it is worlds away from the Bar course, it's just so different because on the Bar course you do civil, which is personal injury mainly, and you do crime – and none of my practice is that. You don't learn about tribunals on the Bar course, you don't learn about legal aid on the Bar course. You would be lucky to get an elective module on immigration law, let alone legal aid and areas that are covered by legal aid and those that aren't. So my practice is dramatically different. Don't get me wrong, I actually think that the Bar course is really useful in terms of teaching you how to do things right.

What the Bar course doesn't teach you, and it's something that you can only learn with time, is how to create your own style and to do things in a way that is persuasive, as opposed to just going through the motions of 'we know this works'; if we put the facts here and the law here and we explain the issues, and that all works. I find, for example, immigration is very different from this because immigration is all about the law but in some of my areas of practice, it's all about the facts. So actually what I learnt at the Bar course, only takes me so far, I'd say.

NB: *I suppose the Bar course prepares you to reach that minimum threshold that you need to be at in order to begin practising. We all start at the very junior end with very junior work, and it's through building things up and gaining confidence and experience that you progress upwards – but practice is all about learning new things, isn't it?*

CB: Absolutely, every day. Learning to fail I think is also really important. On the Bar course you do everything in a really safe environment.

There are failures in the sense of actually failing modules and stuff like that. When I was on the Bar course, there was a general feeling of needing to achieve everything and be super successful and everybody was terrified of making mistakes. What you learn as you go on is that, of course, we all have to take responsibility for our own competence but there is only so much that is actually within your control. There are some things that you just have to accept and you get on with things and you learn to deal with it. Sometimes a tribunal appeal isn't going your way, even when you genuinely thought that it should be, and then you realise that you don't have an appealable decision, which is the most horrible thing, but you learn to get on with that and you learn to survive it. There is so much about it which is so vitally important, but you have to remember also that it's just a job because otherwise it can be all-consuming.

NB: *I agree with that. I think often people can lose sight of the fact that inevitably there comes a point when you must hand the case over to someone else to take it further, whether that's the judge who makes a decision, or the jury who makes the decision. That's when it becomes their responsibility and not yours anymore.*

CB: Yes, exactly.

NB: *Were there any subject areas at university or Bar School that, as you were starting out in your career, you were glad that you took?*

CB: I did the GDL so I did the seven modules over the space of a year and a short introduction to law. Actually, as a housing lawyer, I was pretty glad to have done contract, land law and public law. I think everybody should learn more public law, not less – judicial review, constitutional principles, that sort of thing. It's always really useful to know the ways in which the law can be used to challenge things strategically, and I think you only really get the greatest understanding of that by having some foundation in public law. On the Bar course, there were things that were transferable in the sense of skills such as drafting, advocacy, conference skills. I think I was taught very, very well but I wouldn't say that there was any particular subject matter that I use on a daily basis now. It's more about the skills.

NB: *I want to ask about how your work life has developed and how you describe your work-life balance? When you are not in court for example, do you tend to work on your documents on your computer at Chambers or at home or both?*

CB: Bit of both. I really like being in Chambers. I think Chambers across the country were moving towards remote working before the coronavirus pandemic anyway. I always loved being in Chambers and I think that it's really important for Chambers to consider, moving forward, how we build that environment into remote working. There is nothing better than just having a casual conversation with somebody in Chambers about their work and you actually learn more from that. I can go to my supervisor or any number of members of Chambers. If I just text the housing WhatsApp group and say, 'I need five minutes of somebody's time', there will be somebody available for me to ask my question. What I really liked about being in Chambers is that you just have discussions with people about their cases and it's all those sorts of things that when you have a case of your own, it encompasses some of those issues. You kind of think, I know how to deal with that, or I know how to look for this issue. Sometimes, you just don't know what you don't know, but having those organic conversations with people is a real asset to learning; that's the reason why I went into Chambers regularly.

In terms of work-life balance, I joke when I say I don't have it. I chose not to have a huge amount of work-life balance because I really like my committee work with young legal aid lawyers. I like campaigning. I like getting involved. It's really important to me and I can only feasibly do that outside of my practice otherwise I would just be skint. That said, you can't sustain a legal aid practice without giving yourself respite and without building wellbeing into your routine. You can do it for a year, you can do it for two, but you can't sustain that for 20 years at the Bar. Not in this climate and not with the way legal aid is going.

NB: *If coronavirus weren't here, you would probably spend more time in Chambers working?*

CB: Yes, probably. For me, I really liked that distinction. I like to be able to come home and that being my space to chill, do whatever I like. In terms of people's strategy around wellbeing, that's part of my strategy to maintaining my wellbeing.

NB: *Do you have your own desk and your own room in Chambers or is it hot-desking?*

CB: We hot-desk in Chambers because we are fairly small. We have the floor of a building, and we have four barristers' rooms, but we only have 32 members of Chambers. Everybody is remote working so we actually don't need more space than we have. The people who are in there more regularly will obviously go to their desk because that's a natural thing to do isn't it? But I can sit wherever I want, and I just tend to take my supervisor's desk. He doesn't mind. I hope!

NB: *I wanted to ask about how techy your practice areas are and to what extent you're less paper-based and more digital but I think we have pretty much covered that. When did you last receive a brief in a ring binder?*

CB: I like to be electronic and I have tried really, really hard to build a paper-less practice mainly because of the climate crisis.

NB: *Would you describe practising in your areas of law to be sociable and collegiate, or are you mostly you by yourself?*

CB: It's half and half, though you could say it's me by myself in the sense that when I'm doing immigration and asylum work I tend to be against the Home Office and they don't necessarily have lawyers at every case. The vast majority of times they will have somebody called a presenting officer who is a Home Office employee. I don't have the same relationships with my opposition then, as I might do if I was against a barrister from another Chambers who I knew, but we do have a kind of collegiate environment in the sense that all representatives who appear for appellants in those tribunals are pretty tight, in immigration particularly.

Just to give you an indication as just how rubbish it is in immigration, for a full asylum hearing, you will mostly get a fixed fee for the final hearing. The fixed fee is £302, which sounds like a lot, but the reality is that you get a huge bundle of papers which is usually in the region of 500 to 1,000 pages. You have to write a skeleton argument because, if you don't, woe betide you: the tribunal may well go against you and it will be your fault. You also have to travel regularly. When I was just coming into tenancy at the end of my second six, I would be going to North Shields so I would be travelling four hours or so to get there. By the time I have actually finished the case, I have probably done about 30 hours' work and so I'm getting paid £10 per hour to do it which, if you think about how much you might get per hour in a commercial practice, is off the chart. And you still have to pay your Chambers' expenses which is a certain percent of your earnings.

NB: *Is there a lot of travelling in your work?*

CB: It's pretty common, certainly in an immigration practice. In housing and other areas, probably the furthest I travel is a couple of hours. I do parole boards as well. I once ended up having to go to Haverigg. It took me four and a half hours to get there and some – it's a nightmare by public transport! I try to use public transport wherever possible because again, it's an environmental concern. I ended up driving to Haverigg because there was just no way that I could get there for 10 in the morning with the best will in the world without having to stay overnight in the prison because there wasn't anywhere else.

NB: *What were your expectations before you started in the job about your hours of work and travelling?*

CB: I was fortunate. I knew some people who had done either the Bar course the same year as me, or the year before, who were doing pupillage on Circuit so I already knew that the change was quite major, that there were going to be a lot of hours so I was well prepared for that.

NB: *Wellbeing is something that the Bar Council have a big focus on isn't it at the moment, but it wasn't always so. I was called in October 1994 and wellbeing wasn't on anyone's agenda back then. How do you find that work-life balance in your fields of law, and is your experience the same as that of your contemporaries?*

CB: I think my experience is definitely not the same as my contemporaries because my Chambers builds in wellbeing in the sense that we can have as many papers days as we want and we have control. Even as a pupil, I could still say I would like to have two days out of court a week if I needed it. I never felt a particular pressure to be at work all the time. I have a friend who does commercial law and his pupillage was very different. He had to be in court every day and then he had to do all of his papers around that. For me, that would have been far too much, I couldn't have sustained it. I am very fortunate.

I would say it's all well and good for the Bar to say that wellbeing is important and for people to recognise that it is important, but I think that there needs to be greater implementation of principles of equality and diversity. It is no minor thing because it affects things like allocation of work, fair access to work, all of these sorts of issues. If all Chambers, as should be the case, were compliant with their duties, I think that would have an extraordinary impact on people's wellbeing and would enable us to have more progressive conversations about how we go further, for example by enabling barristers to truly work part-time and building that in as a normal way of working as opposed to something that is exceptionally offered by Chambers. I think that the conversation around all these issues is linked, and for me as a junior barrister it causes me no embarrassment to say that it's tough. I don't always feel adequately supported. This is not because people don't have my best interests in mind, and it doesn't mean that they don't want to change the Bar as much as I do. It's because the pressure doesn't stop when you're a junior barrister. It goes all the way through. The legal system is fighting fires all the time, and the coronavirus period is just one great illustration of that on a massive scale.

NB: *On the topic of diversity and equality, are there any experiences or observations that you can share?*

CB: My experience is sort of two-fold. On the one hand, I am female. I don't know if I would go so far as to say that I have experienced discrimination necessarily, but I am very aware of the fact that in order to be an effective advocate as a female you have to work twice as hard as your male contemporaries and that hasn't changed at the Bar. I am keenly aware that at inquests I tend to be against somebody who is more senior than me and usually a white male. There is absolutely nothing wrong with that, but as a female I then have to really up my game. Often, what I am concerned about and what I always have in my mind is the fact that somebody might be 'playing' me or using the fact that I appear to be a young, female lawyer as some sort of advantage to them, and so that's something that kind of goes with me wherever I go which is part of the reason why I work six days a week. Whilst I'd be cautious about saying I have personally experienced discrimination, there is this imbalance, and it exists and it's real.

It's complicated then by intersectionality isn't it? My experience as a white female lawyer will be very different from other people at the Bar who may experience discrimination on the basis of two or more characteristics, for example skin colour and gender identity. I think we have to have an appreciation not just of general themes but this kind of intersectional analysis of diversity and discrimination.

I have a second side of me which is the side that I don't bring to work so much which is the fact that I'm gay. The reason that I don't bring it to work so much is because I spent quite a long period of time being very scared of what people might say if they knew and not just about what they might say but how they might treat me differently – or not say anything at all which I think is the worst thing. I have had a few bad experiences on mini pupillages where, for example, there was a barrister who was being 'difficult' (of course she was female, and that's the only reason she was being called difficult to begin with) but one of the comments made about this barrister was 'she's always like that because she's a closeted lesbian'. Nobody in the room knew that I was actually a closeted lesbian so they couldn't have ever envisaged the impact that that statement would have on me, but that effectively put me, at the age of 28 or 29, back in the closet and I had been out of the closet for quite some time. It made me terrified of ever bringing it up in conversation and I think these are all things that the Bar has to address. It shouldn't be a matter of me, or anybody else with a protected characteristic, coming to the Bar or coming into Chambers and having to say we have these concerns and having to provide evidence for those concerns. We shouldn't have to be collecting data on issues that we already know exist. The reality is they exist. It would be helpful if the Bar and all Chambers could all just accept what we say about them and then we can move on as a profession. We can work together. I don't want white, straight male barristers to fail. I don't want their power; I just want my own power. I want to have a voice that is heard in this system, and I want to be able to talk about things that are potentially uncomfortable, not because I want to make other people uncomfortable but because the conversation needs to be had.

NB: *Thank you, Ciara. Have you had any thoughts about the future of the Bar in the areas that you work in?*

CB: The future looks pretty bleak, I'd say, for every publicly funded area of practice. I think we are going to have a real issue of retention over the coming years and we will see an exodus of people leaving the publicly funded Bar. I don't yet know how the Ministry of Justice or the Lord Chancellor or the Bar as an institution itself is going to cope with that or even if it is going to be able to mitigate it to be honest. With that in mind, I'm fairly non-committal about the Bar. I didn't come here to be a barrister, I came here because years ago, I ended up in court representing a client that I should never have had to represent. She should never have been in court, and it was horribly unjust. That was the trigger for me pursuing law. I'm a millennial at the end of the day; we are not totally committed to anything, and I can see great benefits to being a paralegal or to working in another field altogether. The reason why I'm here is because I think that there is still an appetite for change, and there are a lot of people that are doing really incredible work and I would like to be part of that and contribute to that if I can.

Postscript:

Since this interview, the Westminster Commission has now published its inquiry into the sustainability and recovery of the legal aid sector (October 2021) which shows the extent of the problems facing junior and aspiring practitioners.

In addition, the government has agreed to remove the means test where funding is available for inquests, which means that bereaved families will not have to pay anything towards their legal costs in limited circumstances. There is still quite a way to go, however, to ensure that bereaved families have access to publicly funded legal representation wherever the state is represented.

6 Crime, Social Mobility

An Interview with Danielle Manson, Garden Court Chambers

NB: *When did you begin tenancy, Danielle?*

DM: Right at the start of lockdown 2019 I had my tenancy interview by video, then I found out the following week.

NB: *Which areas of law have you practised in since beginning tenancy?*

DM: Criminal defence, but I'm hoping in the future to possibly look at actions against the police and maybe inquests, but at the minute it is crime.

NB: *Did you always want to do this?*

DM: In all fairness I probably fell into law being a barrister by mistake – what I mean is that I didn't have a dream when I was 10 or 11 years old that I wanted to be a lawyer. There were things that happened in my personal life that led me to where I am today. When I was 10 my mum was raising me as a single parent because my dad was already in prison and she was arrested and charged with quite a serious criminal offence. She spent about six weeks in custody until she was granted bail. She was a woman of good character, an English teacher. The experience I had of being ripped apart from my mother had a profound impact on me.

I wasn't involved in the trial, my mum wouldn't let me go to court, but obviously I heard a lot about it. It was quite a big case, and she was acquitted. I had positive associations with the lawyers and her legal team and the people that represented her, and so I suppose that was embedded in me from a young age. I think that probably informed my decision to study law at university, and then when I did get there, because of the experience of my mum, I volunteered on the Innocence Project which is where law students look at cases of people who are maintaining their innocence after conviction. It resonated with me because I thought,

DOI: 10.4324/9781003111597-7

well, that could have been our family. If my mum hadn't been acquitted, we possibly would have been campaigning for an appeal and trying to get her out of prison.

I did my law degree, and when you're at university, a lot of 'Magic Circle' law firms come to talk about vacation schemes and the corporate side of things, and that was always very much at the forefront of my mind, but it never really sparked my interest. When I graduated, I went travelling and when I got back from South America I thought I really need to make a decision about what I'm going to do with this law degree that I've got. I hadn't done a mini-pupillage; I hadn't done any marshalling with judges. I was looking for opportunities and I was looking for the mini-pupillages and I looked at the website of Doughty Street Chambers and they had a vacancy for a junior clerk's position. I had just got back from Peru about three days before and I remember just thinking I'll give it a go, and I made an application, got an interview and was offered the job, and so I had to move from Nottingham down to London and start this sort of entry level position in a Chambers.

That was really when I decided that actually this is something that I want to do, and it's when I got the self-belief that I could do it because up until then I sort of knew what the job was but not in a huge amount of detail, so I worked for a year as a junior clerk, photocopying and carrying boxes, et cetera. I was about 25 by that point. I did the Bar course after that and then I worked as a paralegal for a little bit and then started pupillage.

NB: *Wow, that's quite a story.*

DM: It's a funny world, the way things come together. A really quite traumatic experience can shape and form an individual and give them the insight into what needs to be done. What happened to my mum is something that I sometimes talk about with my clients if I'm struggling to generate a rapport with them or if they think that I don't understand what it's like.

NB: *One of the skills I'm teaching at the moment is the skill of how to conduct a conference and how to speak to people let alone how to advise them the content of it but the skills of actually developing a rapport to get the information you need in order to help them.*

DM: I hear some horror stories actually from peers who tell me that they had a conference with a client, and the client was throwing a chair around or got very angry. I'm not saying I do the job better, but I've never been in that position and I often think in this job you need to find a way to manage people, to gain their trust, to manage their expectations; you need to find a way to break through. I've represented clients with severe mental health problems and those who were going through withdrawal from heroin. They've all appreciated that I'm on their side and that I want to secure the best outcome for them. I do think it helps if I mention sometimes what I've been through and show them that I'm not 'the other', that I'm not part of the institution. I'm just an ordinary girl that's doing a job on their behalf.

NB: *It's impressive that somebody from that background can makes it as well as you have done, but in a way it shouldn't be impressive – it should be much easier for people to do that, but it isn't.*

DM: I think that's right. Ultimately part of the problem, the biggest problem, is the financial side of it. I got the Lord Denning scholarship from Lincoln's Inn. They handed me £15,000, and I still wasn't able to afford to do the Bar course full time without having to work. There are probably some people that start and then drop off part way through because they can't manage it. There is a second point. Let's be honest, this is a profession that's shrouded in mystique, you know. Unless you know a barrister or your family has been through the criminal justice system, for example, or the family courts or something, then you wouldn't necessarily have come across this world at all. When young people are looking at possible job opportunities they've got all of that together with the fact that it is an unknown. If you sit down with school kids and you say to them or you can be a barrister – you've got to go to university which costs £10,000 a year for the fees and then your living costs on top of it and you then got to do a one-year course, this, you know, about 20 grand now – students are just going to say thanks but no thanks, I'll do the training contract with a city solicitors' firm because they pay for everything for me upfront. Or I'll be a teacher, or I'll go into politics. I think we lose a lot of the best candidates because of that.

NB: *This surprised me, which perhaps shows how out of touch I was, but a couple of weeks after starting at the university here I saw that there was a notice board where they put up advertisements for pupillage so that students know to apply and there was one Chambers that was offering three chancery commercial pupillages at £65,000 a year. Now that's a phenomenal sum of money to someone starting out as a practitioner in, say, crime. I mean, listen, I've no problem at all with people in chancery who are getting that figure, but it does bother me that capable people have a significant problem to even qualify as a barrister in terms of money and then – once qualified, if they get that* *far – they might go into crime where they can earn a reasonably low amount of money; sure, there is great job satisfaction but right there we see the recruitment and retention problem.*

DM: Absolutely. One of the things that I've learnt in crime is that we're never going to compete with commercial and chancery, like that's the fact. You can make okay money in crime on the big cases if you get a junior brief, or if you get a case that lasts six weeks, you know you'll get you'll get decent money. But at the beginning you're not going to see that work, and it takes a long time to get to that point. I'm the perfect example. I was a pupil for three years in the Magistrates Court earning £50 a day for three years. You push me right to the edge, I'm not actually being paid a great deal and there are all the associated expenses that self-employed people have to deal with. In my case, for example, I pay for my train tickets in advance and, yes, I can claim it back from Chambers but it takes three, four months if I'm lucky to get that money back so then it becomes a cash flow thing because you're constantly paying out every single day to go here there and everywhere – Manchester, Birmingham, Newcastle, Liverpool, I've been everywhere – so it's really important that Chambers have in place the proper systems to support pupils and that they provide travel warrants or they reimburse pupils for travel the same day or the next day.

The nature of the criminal bar is that often you're booking these train tickets at short notice so they are expensive, and it's just not fair for pupils or very junior tenants to fork out for that when ultimately they don't have any say or control over where they're going to work. That was a real nightmare for me. I remember during pupillage at some points not even having money in my bank to sort myself lunch on a long day and having to use the Advantage Card points that I had from Boots to pay for lunch. The job we do is so important and you get huge job satisfaction from it. We want a diverse profession but then the conditions that you are sometimes forced to work within – all of this – are compounded by the fact that the government fails to invest in the court estate. As a defence advocate, you don't have access to facilities at court. I could make myself a really lovely sandwich or some soup or something and take it with me but there's no fridge, there's no microwave. I end up going to Preston spending six pounds on a sandwich and a drink. If you were a clerk with the Crown Prosecution Service you would probably have your own room at court with your own little plug-in kettle, perhaps even a separate kitchen. You go to some courts and they're very well equipped. I was in a Magistrates Court for the first time last week, we'd done a really long trial and prosecution counsel was about to drop, we didn't have time to get any lunch. The court clerk said to us and would you like me to get you a cup of tea and some biscuits. In the back these court staff and the magistrates have little individually wrapped packets of biscuits, I'm sure they've got boxes and boxes of them back there that you know staff and magistrates and CPS could get access to but not independent counsel. We aren't allowed them, but on that day I was, which was brilliant.

NB: *What do you think of the proposed change to opening hours where a courtroom hears two trials, one in the mornings and the second in the afternoons – so-called 'extended operating hours'?*

DM: There was a plan to have a pilot down in London and it was very much kicked to the kerb but now because of Covid it seems to have made a return. Ultimately we need to clear the backlog somehow. I do not have caring responsibilities so I cannot say and I cannot imagine what it would be like if you did have children or an elderly family member. I suppose there is the possibility that it could work favourably if, for example, you could do the school run in the morning, drop your kids off and then take yourself into Chambers, do a little bit of work and be at court for the later sitting and then make arrangements for someone else to pick them up. There's a chance that it could work but, I'll be honest, everything I've read on it tells me that people who do have children or caring responsibilities are saying it's not going to work. We know from what happened during Covid and how we were treated, the courts refuse to list cases for counsel's convenience. If you're a barrister with caring responsibilities and you say, look, I can't do the early system because I have to do the school run, and I just get in for that time but I could do the late sitting because my child goes to an after-school, I could imagine a scenario where the judge says, well we can't fix it for your convenience, I'm afraid, so either come in early or give the case to another barrister. That attitude of being totally ungrateful and unappreciative of all the goodwill that we barristers put into this system day in day out makes people think, actually no I'm not willing to try and make this system work because ultimately it doesn't work for me. There are things that we possibly could do to make it work, but people are at the end of their tether a little bit.

NB: *I agree. It doesn't help at the minute that we're speaking a couple of days after the prime minister gave a speech to conservative party conference saying that we – you, you Danielle – you are 'hamstringing the criminal justice system'.*

DM: This shows total lack of insight into what has actually been happening over the last six months. This is a profession on its knees. We've had years and years and years of cuts, there is a retention crisis and we hit a global pandemic. Instead of holding us up and supporting us and acknowledging the invaluable work that we do, we kick it down. It's not funny, but I don't understand how the government can praise the actions of the police and say look at these police officers who are protectors and who do invaluable work, but at the same time criticise individuals who are part and parcel of the same system that the police work within. What do you think happens to the individuals they arrest? Where do you think they go after the police have done their heroic job and put themselves in harm's way? Well, you've got the prosecutor who will try and keep the streets safe, by opposing bail for example, and then you've got the defence advocate who has to go down and sit in the cell with that same individual that the police officers arrested and who then ensures a fair trial, due process and that everything happens in accordance with the rule of law. Go away, Boris, go away.

It is possible for people from non-traditional backgrounds to overcome the financial hurdles. Firstly there are a number of organisations that really want to help. I've already mentioned Lincoln's Inn who gave me a huge scholarship. The Kalisher Trust also supported me financially when I was given the opportunity to do an internship, and the internship would have otherwise been unpaid and I wouldn't have been unable to do it. During the pandemic, the Barristers' Benevolent Association has been a real lifeline. I like to tell people the names of organisations so that they understand that there are ways to overcome the disadvantage that you're at. The fact that I had to work part-time while studying gave me something interesting to talk about during my interviews. It exposed me to different skills. I tried to tie my part-time work in with law or legal-related activities so for a while I was working as a mentor for an educational charity called Debate Mate. They go into state schools and teach the skill of debate in areas where there are high rates of child poverty. It's all about creating a level playing field so that students that go to ordinary state schools are given the same skills as those that go to Eton and Harrow, the ones that we always see in the Chamber at the University of Oxford who are very accomplished debaters at very young age. I was able to do that alongside studying the Bar course. It was paid quite well and of course it was an incredible experience and actually was something that I talked about in my pupillage interviews. I was asked to give a presentation on a non-legal topic and I chose to talk about Debate Mate and all the incredible work they do. That was at the Chambers that went on to offer me pupillage.

The way that social mobility can be advanced in the profession is through doing things like this and talking about my journey so that hopefully other people read it and are inspired, or at least assured that not everyone is handed everything on a silver platter. With a little bit of hard work and with the support of some incredible organisations you can overcome that hurdle. Just by encouraging people not to self-eliminate is important. I do think that that's a huge problem for social mobility because you get students who go to private school, some of the best schools in the world, who were told from year one that they are the future leaders, the future politicians, future businessmen, the future doctors, dentists, lawyers. In state schools we don't have that same approach, and I think there are some really excellent candidates who lack that confidence when they get to that crucial crossroads: do I put myself in all this debt and do the Bar course or do I just do something a bit a bit safer?

Part of the way we address social mobility is through being very vocal. You know there's the hashtag *IamTheBar* that was trending on Twitter a little while ago that I hope people still search for. The Bar Council's got an initiative where they have social mobility advocates and there are lots of books that have been written by people at the Bar who talk about having come from ordinary backgrounds and overcome what at times feel like insurmountable difficulties.

NB: *We're speaking just a couple of weeks after barrister Alexandra Wilson had that awful experience at a Magistrates Court, not the first time, but three times on the same day when just because she's black she was mistaken for the defendant by professionals.*

DM: Yes, and the public must hear that story and think to ourselves, is this really the sort of profession that I, a young black person, want to go into. Sometimes we don't help ourselves. I think that it's an example of a systemic problem. It all goes back to unconscious bias, this perception about people of colour, black people or XY&Z. I think there are two issues: black people are over-represented as defendants in the criminal justice system and black people are underrepresented when it comes to legal professionals.

NB: *I saw a tweet the other day that the prosecutor, court clerk, district judge and defence counsel in a courtroom were all black women. How strange in a way that in this world that's a remarkable thing and is counted as progress.*

DM: I totally agree. I think that in legally aided work, representation is a lot better. The criminal and family sets are slightly better but still not where they need to be. The QC appointments are quite frankly embarrassing, and the judiciary is even worse.

NB: *Can you give me some examples of the types of cases you are instructed in right now, Danielle?*

DM: I've had lots of drugs matters involving the quite new and interesting Section 45 of the Modern Slavery Act defence arguing that the defendants were involved in the supply of drugs because they've been exploited as part of the county lines gang operation. Some violence, too – Section 18 and Section 20. I'm keeping hold of my Youth Court practice when cases involve a child or young person. I dabbled in firearms as well, so drugs, guns and violence basically.

NB: *In those cases, what sorts of tasks have you had to do?*

DM: In criminal defence, barristers often appear at the first appearances in the Magistrates Court which is usually where the most robust advice has to be given. Usually after the first appearance, the solicitor will take over and then go through the evidence with the client, but when you rock up on a Saturday when someone's been arrested on a Friday night, you're usually the first person they've seen, and you have to give them advice. The court is really cracking down ensuring that entering pleas at the first available opportunity. Often the responsibility is on your shoulders to make sure that if someone should be pleading guilty, they do it at the earliest opportunity so that they get the most amount of credit possible and the lowest sentence.

This has been a little bit more difficult during Covid because if you're having conferences with clients either over the phone or over the video link, I find it a bit harder to generate that rapport and to gain their trust so that they listen to what you have to say. Often the most important thing that they will be thinking about is just getting out of that cell so they might want to enter a not guilty plea just because they don't want to go to prison with Covid looming in the background, even though they should just try and make a bail application.

NB: *Can I ask, have you found the waiting time for video link conferences to prison is excessive?*

DM: Yes. I mean I've been relatively lucky, the majority of my clients are on bail or have been granted bail during Covid. But there are a few where you know the first available conference with the client has been after the trial date! It's been quite difficult.

7 Employment, Planning, Crime

An Interview with Angelica Rokad, 6 Pump Court Chambers

NB: *Angelica, what sort of work have you been involved in since starting tenancy?*

AR: Pupillage was good because I got the opportunity to be involved with lots of different areas so that I wasn't stuck in just one. I had a criminal-based pupillage, but because I am a tenant in a common law set of Chambers, I also got experience of regulatory law, planning law and general civil law. If I was to answer the question of what has happened since I became a tenant, I would probably say that it has changed an awful lot from what I was doing in pupillage, because currently my practice around 60% employment law, about 10 to 15% planning law and the rest is criminal. So, it's sort of turned on its head since pupillage. It has evolved quite a bit.

NB: *It seems that you began doing criminal work mostly and now you do criminal work the least!*

AR: True! You don't plan it, it just happens. My pupillage was about 70% criminal law in terms of work, and for about six months after becoming a tenant, it remained that way. Then, out of the blue, I had one case which was an employment hearing, and after that my employment practice followed. So it's changed quite a bit, all by itself.

NB: *That move to employment law in the main, is that a move that you encouraged when it started?*

AR: Absolutely. I was a volunteer with the Free Representation Unit before pupillage so I had some experience of doing some employment tribunal work. It was something that I already knew about before pupillage and it's something that I encouraged when the opportunity came to me. How it came to me is just pure luck really.

DOI: 10.4324/9781003111597-8

NB: *If you think back to Bar School or even in pupillage, employment law wasn't your destination, then?*

AR: No, I didn't have a destination and that is the truth. It's the reason why I ended up in the Chambers that I did during pupillage. At that stage, I didn't have an area of law that I wanted to specialise in and where I wanted to concentrate all my efforts. Rather, I wanted to experience all the opportunities that I could possibly have. I wasn't really sure that I was set on a specific type of pupillage and so it's evolved organically.

NB: *You say that employment law is most of your work?*

AR: Yes. It really depends on a given month, though. Sometimes, there will be more planning or regulatory work and then maybe some civil instructions which will tip the balance. I think the beauty of it, from my perspective at least, is that I can't tell you here is the exact percentage or tell you that it doesn't change month-by-month or that it doesn't change year-by-year. That's what it's like being a common law practitioner – you never know what's going to happen and turn up in the diary, this year or next year or next month or next week really. I can give you a general indication but that's as best that I can do, I think.

NB: *Yes, I find this at the Bar. Not really knowing exactly what your route is going to be for the next 12 months is partly what makes the job so fun.*

AR: Yes. You could never be sort of, so-called, stuck in a rut, as it were. I don't think that's ever going to happen, and even if you do feel like it's going to happen, there always exists the opportunity to move away and do something different and give something else a go. I think that's the beauty of it. Even if you end up in that position, you will always have the power to try and change something or try something new. I hope that's right for the rest of my practice as well, but you can ask me the question in ten years' time!

NB: *I wonder if you could give me some examples of the types of cases that you are instructed in right now?*

AR: It varies. I am instructed by a local authority to prosecute an unlawful eviction where it is said that the tenants have been harassed by the landlord. That's in the Crown Court and is a multi-day trial involving several witnesses, including children. Often you may think that falls into civil law, but this is purely within the criminal arena.

In another case, I am acting for the local authority which is responding to an appeal against a Planning Enforcement Notice. The local authority has served a Notice on an individual and it has gone to a planning inquiry. On the employment side, I have just finished two fully remote trials last week.

NB: *What sort of issues arose in those remote trials?*

AR: Loads! They couldn't be more different. The first one went ever so smoothly, and the technology worked. My opponent and I were able to deal with issues outside of the tribunal just to try and simplify the process – for example, which witnesses were going to be called first and how we proposed to show the witnesses the electronic bundle when they couldn't have a hard copy in front of them. That was wrapped up in two days. The other one couldn't be further from that experience because we had all sorts of technological issues. We had individuals who couldn't hear us for half of the day nearly. It meant we had to move off into a telephone conference and only part of the trial finished, the rest is still rumbling on to be dealt with on another occasion. It can be really tricky doing remote trials in that sense.

NB: *Are remote trials the future for employment law?*

AR: I think so. I am not sure that every single case will be dealt with remotely or that option will exist for all cases forever, but certainly, I can see merit in cases which are purely about legal submissions dealt with remotely or by telephone. I can also certainly see some merit in a one- or two-day case being dealt with remotely, if there are few witnesses or the issues are fairly narrow, as opposed to that being dealt with at a physical hearing. If your witnesses are sprung far and wide across the country, then it might even be convenient for the parties to appear via remote link. So, I think that's here to stay. Absolutely.

NB: *What sort of law did those two trials involve?*

AR: In both, I was acting for claimants who claimed that they had been unfairly dismissed. Both said that their employer dismissed them either without fair reason or without fair process, or both and then sought an appropriate remedy, namely compensation or their job back.

NB: *Can I ask you about the areas that people study at Bar School, typically? I have three examples: advice, drafting and advocacy, and I wondered, in those cases that we have talked about or indeed others that you have done, was the experience of Bar School useful?*

AR: I think negotiation is certainly something that I have encountered at the court door, for example with my opponent or perhaps even negotiating with a client. Sometimes you're trying to present what you think is likely to happen in the most user-friendly way and, whilst that isn't really negotiation, you are trying to explain your view of what's going to happen and try to get somebody to understand someone else's point of view – be it the other side or even the (likely) view of the judge. In terms of advice, advocacy and drafting, I would absolutely say that I do all three. I was in and out of court every day in my second six and even in tenancy, about three or four days out of the working week I was in court. Then there's also written advocacy which is not to be underestimated. For example every time you draft a document, you are not just using your drafting skills, you are applying your advocacy skills in writing. So, in Bar School, you traditionally refer to drafting as starting of legal claims and procedures, but drafting, I think, is much wider in its application in practice.

NB: *Do employment judges ask that counsel draft the orders for the judge then to approve or does this come exclusively from the judges?*

AR: Usually, practitioners don't get involved in drafting the order. They might comment on the wording of an order, if, for example, any comments are sought by the judge or are particularly important from the perspective of the client. It is usually a collaborative approach between all the parties and in front of the judge. For example, in the trial I finished the other week, there was comment sought by the judge about how a particular order for disclosure should be framed: what would be too broad; what would be too narrow? But then, having heard submissions from both parties, the judge made a decision and was responsible for drawing up the order.

NB: *I often think that the need for, and the importance of, written advocacy can be underestimated. People think of advocacy as being the voice speaking which, of course, it is, but written advocacy can get you 70% of the way there.*

AR: I agree. I think at the start of my career I certainly underestimated the power and role of written advocacy. That is probably a common misconception because we all watch legal dramas on television, and nobody films the barrister drafting their closing submissions! But this profession is not only about what you say but how it translates on paper, and if you have got a succinct and clear style of written drafting, your points are almost made for you. I certainly think we both might have experienced instances where you might offer to assist the judge, sometimes the judge says: 'Actually, having read your written submissions, I think I've got the point you're trying to make'.

NB: *Those remote cases that we discussed a moment ago, are those typical of your practice so far? It seems, from what you are saying, they probably are?*

AR: Yes, they are. I started off in my second six with trials in the Magistrates' Court. They were my bread and butter. Also during pupillage, I did have the chance to go to the Crown Court. In fact, my first actual appearance before a court was at Woolwich Crown Court, with an instruction late the evening before! But I've had experience of being a trial advocate in the Crown Court during pupillage and in tenancy. I didn't get involved in doing planning inquiries as sole counsel during pupillage – I think they would be a bit complex at that stage – but certainly what I have described is typical of my practice as I see it, currently.

NB: *What is involved in a planning inquiry?*

AR: The ones I usually deal with concern enforcement notices issued by the local authority to respond to a breach of planning law (for example). If you are acting for the local authority, you then would be responding to an appeal made by the individual who has been served with the notice, and the appellant would be arguing that the notice is unsatisfactory in some respects and should be quashed, or that notwithstanding the breach of planning law, the inspector should grant permission for the building to stand. However, there are other cases that I have been involved with where I have been led as a junior, which are different because they involve broader issues and aren't related to an enforcement notice. For example, if planning permission is given for the building of 500 or 1,000 houses, and there many aggrieved residents or perhaps environmental concerns or air quality concerns, then a planning inquiry becomes a much larger (and longer) affair. It depends.

NB: *This brings us nicely on to talk about the sorts of people or organisations who have largely been your clients. You have talked about local authorities and also individuals in the employment sphere who make an unfair dismissal claim.*

AR: Yes. Honestly, I hope I am not doing a disservice by saying it's broad, because it really is. It would not be unusual for me to have a varied day. On Monday, I could be acting on instruction from the Crown Prosecution Servicel; Tuesday, acting on behalf of a private individual having received instructions from a local solicitor's firm; Wednesday receiving instructions from a local authority, and so on. The beauty of it is that I am not limiting my instructions to one area, or one specific individual or type of public body, or even private body.

NB: *Yes. I think that's probably the key to practice these days, having a broad base, perhaps more so than in previous times. Having a diverse client base is important because in terms of career progression we can't know whether the amount of work in one area might decrease in time, and if we have focused on that exclusively, we might be in trouble then?*

AR: Absolutely. Especially , you can't get better experience than working for different clients in different areas that you are interested in. I have always approached it that way. My approach to cases is to think, if I was on the other side what would I say? If I was acting for the claimant and not respondent, what would I say? If I was prosecuting and not defending, what would I say? And I think that makes for better advocacy because you know what points your opponent is likely to raise and you can deal with them. Also, it just makes the whole experience much more practical because you're not boxed into a specific area that you may do day in and day out.

NB: *What about your case load? What it has been like in tenancy and how has it compared with your second six?*

AR: I think it's important to set this the context of Covid-19, because had I been asked this question beforehand, my answer would have been different. I was always very busy in second six, as I am now. The amount of times that I appear in court haven't really changed, albeit now, I have more remote hearings than before because of the global pandemic. In terms of how it's changed during Covid-19, it's very difficult to say because there was a period during the first lockdown where all of a sudden cases just weren't coming through and workload did definitely drop compared to what my workload was like before. If I was to answer the question based on my current experience, I'm advising on at least six to seven cases on sort of a given week or two-week period, whether that means I am going to be in court or whether that means I am doing something in writing. I think it's very easy when you enter this profession to think: 'Well I'm in court, so that means I have got one case and if I'm in court two times a week, I have got two cases'. The reality is that you are always doing work for cases that are maybe even months, sometimes years, down the line and you might even be doing work for cases that turn up at 8pm the day before the hearing. In terms of planning the case load, it's very difficult. You need to be organised. What I think is important to note is that you are always going to be juggling a few balls at the same time. It gets better with practice.

NB: *The next question is about the percentage of your time that you typically spend in court or other tribunals versus working at your desk.*

AR: If I was to answer this question based on how things stand currently, going in Chambers is a little bit limited given Covid-19. Prior, I would be in court three to four times a week, but I would also go into Chambers after I was in court that day or possibly even on the day that I wasn't in court, just to do some papers. So, I would be in court three or four times a week and I would be in Chambers doing paperwork three to four, possibly even five, days a week to be honest.

NB: *Do you mostly work on papers or documents in Chambers or at home, or could it be both?*

AR: Before the pandemic, I was always working in Chambers as opposed to at home, mainly for two reasons. One, I was already out in court probably, so it would be easier to come back to Chambers and finish off the paperwork, put the files back, take the new ones for the next day. Two, Chambers has a collegiate atmosphere, and it is great to be there. Sometimes you walk into Chambers and you would just want to get a specific piece of work done, but very often you go to Chambers to catch up with colleagues, to see how their day was and to share how your day was. And sometimes, you have a question that you know someone in Chambers will be able to help with. It might not even be a legal question, it might just be a question about tactics. So, in terms of how I spent my time, a lot of the time was in Chambers but since the pandemic, it has been converted to working from home but also having my colleagues at the touch of a button on my phone.

NB: *This is when I would normally ask about the sorts of courts or other tribunals that you attend, but actually we have talked about that already. The Crown Court obviously is a wig and gown job, but I don't think anything else is that you go to, is it?*

AR: No, it would just be the Crown Court actually. If you are going to an Appeal Court, then you would of course have your wig and gown in most cases. I was recently in the High Court, but being virtual and from home, there wasn't even wigs and gowns then! But everything else I do, there are no wig and gowns.

NB: *Do you miss that?*

AR: I get to don my wig and gown every time I go to the Crown Court which is a couple of times a month maybe, so, I'd like to say I do still have the option to put it on but sometimes you won't put it on for a month and you do miss that bit.

NB: *What parts of your practice do you find the most interesting and are there any areas that some people may find less exciting?*

AR: Across the board I'd like to say that the thing that's great is you are given a fairly knotty problem, especially in the planning or employment side of my practice. It could be a problem that's grown worse over a number of months, or a number of years even, and somebody is coming to you to find out what's the most practical, cost-effective, efficient solution to resolve it. The job can be quite literally working out what the best solution is without having to go to court. It's great to be involved in a problem where your input helps resolve a thorny issue that's been dragging on a while. In terms of what's interesting and what's not, there are always cases which start simple but then turn very complicated really quickly. I would be lying if on those occasions you don't have a thought to yourself where you think: 'I wish I didn't have to do this!'. The other thing which potential entrants might want to bear in mind is the sheer travelling time. That is an area which I underestimated in terms of how exhausting it can be and in terms of how you plan your life around what you're doing Monday to Friday or even indeed on the weekend. Possibly also, it's the not knowing that people may find difficult. You may find out what you're doing the next day at 6pm, 7pm and 8pm the night before. A couple of months ago I was waiting at the end of the phone at 8pm with my clerk wondering whether or not I was going to go to Manchester the next day. That slowly becomes normal but I certainly think others looking into the profession are a bit shocked at how late in the day your next day can shape up.

I don't know whether my clerks will be happy with me sharing this story, but I feel compelled to share it! I had just finished a full-day trial and had literally stepped onto the platform at Euston station, only four stops to home. The next day, I had lined up a paper day as I had a complicated trial to prepare for and I really needed to concentrate on the papers. As I stepped off the train at Euston, I got a call from my clerk to say: 'You won't believe it, but one of the jury trials that we thought was not going to happen has been called in by the Crown Court at the last minute and it's starting 10am tomorrow at Harrow'. It was a planning trial which I hadn't done before but which I really wanted to have a go at, so it was a bit of a rough choice. I think by that point it was then 7pm. The papers came at 8 or 9pm, and a colleague in Chambers was kind enough to run through it with me. I got home, had dinner, crammed, and then went off to Harrow the next day and started opening the trial at 10am. Going back to the previous question, those are the less exciting possibly less glamorous parts of this job. But you muddle through, don't you. You find a way.

NB: *We talked about the case, the planning inquiry where you had been led, I think you said. What sort of tasks have you done when you have been led?*

AR: I have been led in quite a few cases. They have all been in planning law. In one, I was led by a silk in Chambers who had a ten-day planning inquiry which centred on whether a huge housing development should be built on an area of land which was designated as a high-risk flood zone, in short whether the appellant should get permission to build these rather large houses on that land. We were acting for the Environment Agency.

NB: *What did you actually do as the led junior?*

AR: Well, the Environment Agency was an interested party. That meant that was there was a lot of groundwork that was already done between the appellant and the local authority but which the Environment Agency wasn't privy to. There was a lot of catching up to do! First, we had to collate all the papers from the two years that this case had been running to understand what had happened. I sat down with my leader and summarised the developments that had happened, getting a hold on the timescale and identifying what issues need to be resolved now before we started speaking to our clients. I had a lot to do with the drafting of written closing submissions and cost submissions. I was also able to go out on the site and produced a set of questions that needed to be asked of the relevant individuals. There was a conference with the Environment Agency – several conferences in fact – where the relevant questions needed to be identified, prepared and then summarised for my leader.

NB: *Great. Can we look at your expectations about the job, and whether what you have ended up doing has matched what you previously thought it would be. I wonder if you thought that Bar School, for you, prepared you for what your practice is now?*

AR: In some respects I think I was very fortunate before starting a Bar course and starting pupillage to have met a few mentors who really took me under their wing. In terms of how it's adapted since being in practice, I think I underestimated how many different things you would have to do on a given day all at the same time. You are being pulled in all different directions to the point where you're sitting in a tribunal or you're in court and during the break, you will be writing up an e-mail or drafting a document in an unrelated area of law for a different solicitor and a different client for the next day, the next week, the next month;l and you will be doing many different things at the same time. I think I underestimated the late instructions that come with the job and sometimes you don't get the luxury of having lots of time to think about a case. What that means is that you've got to be very efficient in your practice and you have to identify at the outset whether you can or you can't commit to an instruction. Sometimes – often really – that means sacrificing a personal commitment that you have. Try and get some very understanding friends and family! That's an element which I think you have got to have: a very forgiving support network.

NB: *I agree. It seems to me there are two parts of practice that when I was at Bar School, I didn't realise how important they were, and they very much related to what we have been discussing. Firstly, Bar School for me back in 1994 had an element to it called 'fact management'. They gave you typically a massive bundle of documents and said, here you are, and you had to prepare it for your pupil supervisor, not knowing anything about it, so you had to familiarise yourself with all the papers and organise them, structure them, and list what you thought your pupil supervisor should be considering first, and that was massive, took me absolutely ages and I didn't do it very well but that's such good preparation for what we need to do. Also, the second part of it, which I suppose is the same thing said in another way, is learning how to target your reading and your understanding. I think that whenever you're faced with a time-pressured case you make sure you're aware of what you need know first; and if there is something that you don't need to know right now, you can look at that later.*

AR: I entirely agree with you. Managing your time and managing your time with other people is really, really important. I think those pressures are even more live when you are dealing directly with your client. The majority of the time, you have your client with you. It's their case, and they want to make sure that you, as their representative, have all the relevant facts that they think might be relevant. There has to be an element of managing the amount of facts which you can deal with at a given point in time. You could ask a thousand questions of your client and get a thousand different good answers which might be relevant to what you need to do, but you need to know what the right questions are to ask, and you need to know when an answer that demands a bit more of an enquiry. I think that this is a skill that you only really develop once you are in practice. It is really hard to teach somebody that.

NB: *Were there any subject areas at university or Bar School that you took and then later when you started practice, you were very glad that you did?*

AR: Well my university made all its students take part in a moot in the first year. All of them. I am very grateful for that because in all honesty if I hadn't done that moot I don't think I would be doing this job. It's the first chance I got to try and do something comparable in a student setting. At Bar School, I had the opportunity to do an advanced civil module. It was just an enhancement on the ordinary civil module which Bar students take. That module was really helpful because when you start at Bar School, you are given these huge practitioner textbooks that you have never seen before and you think to yourself: 'What on earth am I meant to do with this?'. It's only when you have a look at a problem back in real life and you must identify what the relevant paragraph might be in this huge textbook that you start to do the work which you would do in practice. So, I think the more practise I had at that, the better. That was certainly something I got from the advanced civil course, yes.

NB: *I know one option I took at Bar School was the course dealing with drug trafficking. In all honesty, I really struggled with the concepts of that at Bar School because it seemed so opposite to the main features of criminal law. I didn't do very well but, looking back, the fact that I did so badly with it then meant that when I later came to do it in practice, I came to understand it more, in particular the different thinking required. I probably had to get it so wrong first in order to get it right later.*

AR: Yes. That makes perfect sense. One example of the things I did in my second six was driving disqualification hearings in the Magistrates' Court where you know somebody has effectively become a totter – in that they get so many points on their driving licence that they end up at risk of being disqualified for a given period of time. The first time that you do it, it's really, really hard because you have to know where do you look? Where do you start? You have been given somebody's personal facts. What's relevant? What's not? Everybody who you probably represent in one of those cases says, I am at risk of losing my job, my livelihood, if I am banned from driving. That sounds very compelling the first time that you hear it, but then you delve a little bit deeper and you realise that what the law says is – in summary, those things don't always amount to a reason not to disqualify you. And so the first time you do it, it's really tough, but then you do more of those cases over time and you just learn more and more so it doesn't faze you as it might have done before.

NB: *Can we talk about the most difficult changes that you have got used to? We have talked about this in a sense because there are the other parts of the job that aren't law, like the travelling.*

AR: The things that I have found very tough especially during second six when I had not only my own cases that I was doing as a pupil, but also I did have requests from my supervisors to do jobs and tasks for them and possibly other members of Chambers as well. It was very difficult and I did the best that I could. It doesn't stop when you're in tenancy because you might not have your supervisor and you won't do work for other members of Chambers, but you will have to deal with the task of managing your own practice and developing clients and promoting yourself. That's really tricky at the start. You will always have many, many other things that you need to do at the same time. I am one of those people that has a 'to do' lists and I write them down on a piece of paper and then I get to cross them off when I do it and no matter how hard I try, there will always be something left outstanding and it will grow the next day! It's very hard knowing that you will not have a complete checklist at the end of a day, on a Friday or even the working week. At the end of the day, you might have even more tasks than those that you crossed off. Everybody at the Bar is very supportive, though, in making sure that you are not too overwhelmed and there's always someone at the end of the phone if you need them. So, there is access and there is support available, you have just to be very strict with yourself as well.

NB: *We are coming on to your work life, how it's developed, your work-life balance and whether you tend to work in Chambers or at home.*

AR: I work usually in Chambers, we have what's called the junior library. Members of Chambers who are sort of around my call but who don't have our own room sit there. We do have a very large area there with a desk that you can drop into as and when you need to after court. That has been so helpful because often it will be those members of Chambers who will have experience of the question that you are trying to get to the bottom of.

NB: *How techy are the practice areas that you work in?*

AR: I'd like to say that I'm quite good. Before the pandemic, I would be one of those people who would print out the bundle, I would highlight it, I would flag up different areas with a post-it note and I'd have everything in a hard copy because inevitably somebody will turn up at the hearing and perhaps they are missing a page or perhaps they have forgotten their witness statement or perhaps the bundle hasn't made its way to the court and you can assist. Because of the pandemic, though, things have moved more remote. When I did my first fully remote trial, it was the first time I actually used a bundle electronically so I hadn't printed off anything. I think any budding barrister could take from this pandemic that that's an element of remote technology that's here to stay.

NB: *How would you describe your typical hours of work?*

AR: How long is a piece of string! It really is one of those questions. I know this sounds not very believable really, but honestly, you could have a day where you think: 'I'm going to court and I'll be there all day and then I'll finish, go home, have some dinner and it's the weekend'. And something might happen that's entirely unrelated to what you do which is perhaps there wasn't enough time to hear the case that you have prepared, or that somebody didn't turn up who was a crucial witness and then what happens is your case goes short and what you thought was going to be whole day in court, ends up being maybe even an hour, if that. Or vice versa, you could end up in court for a lot longer than what you expected – that's more usual than finishing early! In terms of actual hours though, if I was to sort of average it all up, I generally aim to be in court by 9am if I have got a 10am hearing. That will involve me often travelling before getting into court at 9am which often means I am up by at least 7am. Things have changed with the pandemic but generally, that's how it is with travel. I would generally expect to finish court around 4.30, possibly 5pm, depending if that's a full day. Even if it's a half day, I end up going back to Chambers, having lunch with some colleagues or lunch on the way there. I generally aim to leave Chambers about 6pm, and I tend to do a couple of hours' work at home. There will always be those days when sometimes I'm leaving Chambers at, say, 11pm or later. Maybe some weekend work – it's difficult to predict.

NB: *Do you do a lot of travelling?*

AR: Absolutely. My practice is spread over the South East so it's not uncommon for me to catch the fast train from Kings Cross, St Pancras to Folkestone, to Maidstone, to Canterbury. It can be an hour and a half travelling there in the morning, an hour and a half travelling back in the evening, then there will also be the travel I have got to factor in to go to Chambers. Then you have got to come back from Chambers so, overall, at least four hours I'd say travelling in a day.

NB: *What were your expectations of the travelling before you started?*

AR: I did all my mini-pupillages in London and I lived in London. I wasn't expecting it to be so tiring, but it is, especially when you have been travelling for four to five hours a day, five days a week. There is an element of just, you know, sitting down on a Friday and not actually wanting to do anything – just have dinner and go to bed and that's just perfect really, an ideal world!

NB: *Wellbeing is a real thing now with the Bar Council but certainly it wasn't always. How do you find sort of work-life balance in the areas that you work in?*

AR: It's something which I hadn't actually factored in. As I have gone into tenancy and developed my own practice, I am managing my workload with my clerks. I will not take a case on if I feel I can't commit to it because of the hours I am already doing or perhaps there will be those occasions where you have got this brilliant case you would really enjoy doing, but you have got a really important personal occasion to commit to and you have simply just got to be there for that day. I have become more responsible and honest with my clerks now. I would really encourage people to have an eye on that. It's really difficult when you're starting out because you might think to yourself: 'I have got to do the best I can, I have got to do as many cases as I can, I want to be busy, I want to be working with my colleagues and doing exciting cases'. That's great and it's what everybody aims to do as well, but there will come a point in time where you think, actually, I want to go on holiday and I need a break. You will always be doing something even if it's replying to an e-mail about a case that's happening a month off (even when you're on holiday) because somebody needs the answer to their question and you are trial counsel.

NB: *Can we come to the topic of diversity? Have there been any experiences or do you have any observations about diversity at the Bar? Sex equality, race equality, social mobility and any other topic that you think touches on any of those.*

AR: Speaking from personal experience, I had no lawyers as family members or friends. Nobody in my family, especially when I was growing up, knew any barristers at all and, as I said, the only reason I am doing what I'm doing now is because my university made all students take a moot as part of their assessment and that's where it all started for me.

In terms of social mobility, I am of the view that it's still very difficult to enter this profession, to even get an idea of what it's like at the Bar, to see if it's the right profession for you before you commit to it – mainly because of the financial burden of entering the profession in the first place. I was really lucky to get a scholarship from my Inn, Middle Temple. I am very grateful for that. I think it is a topic which it deserves continual coverage because I don't think the Bar has got there yet in terms of social mobility.

My story isn't even the most difficult story that you hear. There are many more individuals who are at the Bar who have given up a lot to be where they are. There are great initiatives around, for example the scholarship scheme that I have mentioned from the Inn and individual Chambers in the way that they approach recruitment, for example. I am of the view that unless and until we sort out the big money question, how it is we fund the Bar and how it is we get here, then it will never be resolved.

NB: *Have you experienced yourself any issues with sex equality that you want to talk about? Let me give you an example I came across just yesterday on Twitter about a barrister who was a young lady barrister appearing before a judge who she respected and liked – but who called her 'young lady' throughout the hearing, and that's neither acceptable nor professional on any level.*

AR: No, absolutely. That is really poor, and there is an appropriate term to be used for any representatives that are gender neutral which is 'counsel'. The fact that we hear real live stories as of today just goes to show that it's still an issue that crops up. I personally haven't had a comparable story or an example to give but that really is not to say that those issues aren't there.

NB: *Often students do ask about what sort of income progression through the early years they might expect if they came into any particular area of law. Can you help with that?*

AR: First of all, it will depend on the area that your pupillage is in and even the type of work within that area that your Chambers might do. So, for example, if I take the area of crime, that may involve legally aided work. But even from there, you could have a criminal set which practises in private appellate work or acting for private individuals and then that's different to legally aided work. Everything depends on the type of work that you might do within that area and who your clients are.

NB: *Well, I wonder whether we can approach in a more general way which is kind of somebody practising mainly in employment law, let's say five years into tenancy. Is there a sort of idea that can be given about the sort of income that they might expect?*

AR: I don't know because sometimes even in employment, for example, you may be acting for a claimant, and if so, you are just maybe dealing with somebody who has been unfairly dismissed from work who is trusting you with their savings or a source of savings from another individual perhaps, often family members. You might not have the same level of access to resources or funds than the respondent does. You might have a client that has an insurance policy or legal expenses cover, but you have also got to factor in that there are policy limits to every cover, the money isn't endless, it's not out there for general consumption, it's there for specific reason. The other thing which I think is important is that parties are always trying to resolve their differences, or they should be as best they can. The worst-case outcome for them or sometimes, is the fact that they are going to trial over this matter which could be resolved more amicably.

NB: *How do you see the future? At this stage of your career do you have got any thoughts at all about what the future will be like?*

AR: It's important to emphasise that the pandemic has really changed how I thought my year would pan out and even the years going forwards. I never thought at the start of this year I would ever do a trial over remote technology, I just didn't even think that was possible, quite frankly. Things have changed but this profession is adaptable.

NB: *When you're my age, which is 50 (say it quietly), assuming that you haven't made it onto the bench by then, do you think you will still be practising in this field?*

AR: I would like to say so. I hope so. It's been great. There are always those days where you think: 'I'm so tired, I don't want to do this *right* now'. But it's all on you so you find the time to do it anyway. Despite all the hard times, there has never been a day where I think that I want to do something else. If you stop enjoying it, then that's the sort of trigger point to maybe thinking that you won't be doing this work forever but certainly, my experience so far, whilst it's not all been what it looks on TV, I'm very happy to have made it here and very happy to stay. I still hope I am here in, whenever it is, 20, 30 and 40 years. You can ask me that question again and I wonder whether I've had one too many sleepless nights by then!

8 Commercial Law

An Interview with Sophia Dzwig, 3 Verulam Buildings

NB: *When did you start your tenancy, Sophia?*

SD: I started tenancy in October 2018 having done pupillage there in 2017/2018.

NB: *Which areas of law have you practised in since you began your tenancy?*

SD: Broadly commercial law, which is any dispute really involving a business. Largely the disputes are variations of civil fraud and they can encompass insurance disputes, financial disputes, banking disputes, bribery and many other different things. They have been the core parts of my practice.

NB: *Are they typically contractual disputes?*

SD: They can be, there is often a contractual element to them. In fairness the work that I do in my own smaller, unled cases, tends to have some kind of contractual or tortious basis but it's a lot of misrepresentation, some of it alleged to be fraudulent.

NB: *Is this the sort of work that you always wanted to do?*

SD: I wasn't somebody who always wanted to be a lawyer. My mum is a lawyer, but I didn't want to be a lawyer. I started thinking about it properly at university when I was doing a non-law degree and had a third year out. I was doing a four-year degree and did some work in a law firm. I also did a lot of mini-pupillages and really enjoyed those, so I signed myself up for the GDL conversion course and then a Bar Course, and then pupillage, and here we are!

When I came to Chambers, I didn't think civil fraud would be what I ended up doing. Chambers traditionally has a reputation for being a

DOI: 10.4324/9781003111597-9

very, very strong banking and finance set, but actually its work is much, much broader than that. Really most of the banking and finance work I've done is my own smaller cases.

NB: *It's interesting to hear that you did a non-law degree. I went to a careers fair at a big school a few weeks ago. It surprised me how many people didn't know that you don't have to do a law degree. It's just a natural assumption to think that you should do law if you want to be a lawyer.*

SD: I spent my third year in Italy, and there you have to study law at undergraduate level otherwise you cannot be a lawyer, but I'm eternally grateful that we don't because I got to do what I really enjoyed at university and I would never have chosen law.

NB: *I know we are digressing a bit. I did the first year of the German law degree in my third year at university and just as you describe for Italy, you have to do a substantial number of years at university.*

SD: Then it is the same that you can go straight into the judiciary?

NB: *Yes, you can. It's a career choice.*

SD: But then they probably think having magistrates deciding cases without legal training is completely mad!

NB: *Can I ask you, how would you describe the splits in the types of work that you do at the moment?*

SD: All the work that I do is commercial work but that really does cover a huge range of disputes so, that could be a contractual claim just between two businesses, a banking claim, an insurance claim. I have been doing a lot recently in insurance which is where my practice has gone. That is not even very normal in Chambers. I am doing a dispute over some stolen artwork.

NB: *What are banking cases about?*

SD: My very first hearing as a second six pupil was somebody who had received a cheque that wasn't meant for them, and the bank was trying to get it back. A case I'm doing at the moment is a multi-million-pound private banking dispute where somebody was forced to sell a portfolio of assets due to the market crashing last spring, and they say if the bank had done what they wanted several years before, that wouldn't have been the case and so they are claiming damages. Banking covers a whole range of cases. You might class banking cases as civil fraud with a financial aspect because of the nature of the underlying fraud. I have been involved in a case for the last three years where the Danish tax authority says that securities trading was a fraud on the tax authority, but they are not suing in tax law, they are suing in civil fraud. There are a lot of people from my Chambers in that dispute.

NB: *Can you give some examples of the types of cases that you are instructed in right now? I guess we have just touched on one which is the artwork case?*

SD: That's actually a case unled; I am doing it by myself. I am advising an auction house which sold some items which turned out later to have been stolen. I'm advising them. I mentioned the Danish tax authority case. I am doing a case about the portfolio of securities that were sold when the market crashed last spring. I'm doing a couple of arbitrations. One arbitration is based in Hong Kong; an insurance one about whether again some circular trading is covered under a policy.

NB: *When you saying you are doing an arbitration, what does that mean?*

SD: Arbitration is a private dispute resolution mechanism. These are parties that are based in Singapore and China. They have decided to arbitrate which means they are not going through the courts. In this case, they are going through the Hong Kong International Arbitration Centre (HKIAC) which supplies them with a set of procedural rules to follow, as you would in court, and they have chosen a panel of three Hong Kong and English judges. We have Hong Kong solicitors and counsel who are all in England. I am doing another arbitration, this one based all in England which is an unfair prejudice petition under the Companies Act, wealthy shareholders who have fallen out with each other. They own a company together and the claimant is saying that the acts of the others are unfair to him and that he should be either bought out, or should be able to buy them out, of the company. Those are examples of just some of the cases I am doing at the moment.

NB: *Am I right I thinking that when you enter into an arbitration such as you have described, you are bound by the arbitration ruling so it's a bit like a court?*

SD: Yes, you are bound, and often there isn't an avenue of appeal which I think is something a lot of people don't realise. Some parties might find it frustrating, but some parties do not. It means that no matter what the legal merits of the decision, whether you agree with it or not, it's the decision. It might not be much quicker than a court but at least you don't have the prospect of years and years of appeals. There are very limited grounds on which arbitrations can be appealed under the Arbitration Act 1996.

NB: *Do people undergo arbitration not just for finality but also because it's cheaper than going to court?*

SD: It's not necessarily cheaper or quicker than court. It is, however, private. So in the case of these shareholders who have fallen out, if it were known that there was a huge dispute going on, and if it weren't behind closed doors, that could affect the price of the business. So that's an example where privacy is very, very important to them. For all sorts of reasons, parties might not want their dirty laundry aired in court and arbitration is very appealing for that reason.

NB: *What sort of tasks have you had to do in your cases and arbitrations? You will remember Bar School of course, and the learned skills of advising, drafting and advocacy. Do you deploy those skills?*

SD: Some of what I learnt during my time at Bar School has been particularly useful. In particular, having a good grounding in the Civil Procedure Rules [CPR]; that's really important and gives you an advantage. Coming to the Bar straight from Bar School where you have been learning CPR does help because you know your way around the rules. Likewise, I found for the kind of smaller banking cases that I do where I go to the County Courts, or much smaller cases in the High Court by myself, I do a lot of summary judgment applications which are a mainstay of civil advocacy in Bar School. That is work where a dispute is said to have no real prospect of success one way or the other, and the claimant or defendant can ask for the dispute to be resolved without trial. I have done a lot of those.

NB: *What about drafting specifically? Some advocates I have spoken to of course draft particulars of claim an awful lot. Is that something that you do?*

SD: We don't have to do it all that often because quite a lot of the disputes we do are very long-running. You are not doing them week in, week out, because that's not the timeline of your cases. That said, I have been drafting a pleading in the unfair prejudice petition that I talked about. It was an arbitration defence which is a little bit different. It is more or less in the same style as a court pleading in this case save for the fact that it was hundreds of pages – too long to be allowed in court. Likewise, I did an amended defence, again with a leader, earlier this summer and I have a small case of my own as well which I pleaded over the summer. When I say small, it's about a loan for £290,000 which in finance terms is small. It's something I do, but you can go for months without doing one. It's actually something that pupils want to have more experience of because it's not the easiest skill.

NB: *What about opinion writing?*

SD: I do a lot of advising. It doesn't always take the style of a formal opinion. It's more or less always written advice. I don't give very much oral advice myself. If you have a conference over the phone or Zoom or Teams these days, it's quite often a Silk advising for my cases. So I may have done the background research and some background drafting but actually advising in conference tends to fall to somebody more senior. A lot of my work is legal research which involves writing a note or an Advice which either informs your Silk's Advice in conference, or it becomes an e-mail to the solicitors. If you're on an on-going case, there is a lot more ad hoc advice. You are sometimes asked to advise on issues rather than the merits of a whole dispute. But then twice earlier this summer I have done formal opinions with a leader on insurance disputes so, again, it's mixed.

NB: *What sorts of people or organisations have largely been your clients – apart from millionaires?*

SD: Because of the cost of High Court proceedings, a lot of my clients are either very wealthy individuals or companies. In the smaller cases, to employ somebody at my level in the County Court, for example, you are quite often being instructed by a company that cannot represent itself but is dealing in a small dispute when you might well be against a litigant in person in your first few years. You are still representing a company, but the interaction is very different when you have got a litigant in person on the other side.

NB: *What has your case load been like in tenancy and how did that compare with your second six?*

SD: I was on my feet in my second six which is unusual in a commercial set but 3VB, because it has that traditional finance banking practice, has a lot of these small cases where you go along for a bank and you do a very small summary judgment application. That can be your bread and butter. I was not in court every day; that's just not how a commercial practice works. I think I did four to six hearings in my second six months, each lasting maybe an hour, and that's a decent number for a commercial set.

NB: *It never ceases to surprise me how practice in different areas varies so much. It's very different than, say, a criminal pupillage, where you would be in court every morning and afternoon probably.*

SD: In my second six I also did work for my supervisors. We have four supervisors in Chambers doing pupillage which is quite normal for a civil set. I had my last two supervisors for the first half and second half of my second six. In the first half I was predominantly doing work for my supervisor although I did a few small appearances by myself. They continued to assess me and at the end of that seat was my tenancy decision. After that I was predominantly doing my own work. I had a case representing an oligarch, there was me and two Silks. I didn't really do much work at all for my fourth seat supervisor although they were an invaluable 'backstop and common-sense check' and a source of advice. I was still sitting physically in their room in Chambers which is how a pupillage works. You are still quite protected in that sense. Your workload typically goes up as a tenant.

NB: *We have already touched on the percentage of time that you spend in court or other tribunals or hearings. How much time do you spend working at your desk?*

SD: It is mostly working at my desk. I have a hearing on 15 October 2021 by myself but my last proper appearance in court by myself was in January 2020 because of adjournments during Covid. I have had a lot of hearings where I'm led. I had a very busy stint in January/February last year where I was in court on the same case, I think it was ten to twelve times in three weeks doing injunctions which is where you go along and you ask the court to urgently stop somebody else or make somebody else do something.

Then I was in this very big Danish tax authority case where we had a case management conference almost every month for the whole year. It was due for a four- to six-week preliminary issue earlier this autumn and a four-term trial in 2023/2024. it needed a lot of case management, so I was in court every month last year on that case and early this year for those hearings, and subsequent to that, actually it's all been paperwork since March. We had a four-day preliminary issue trial in March and consequentials in April which are follow-ons from a major hearing where you decide what happens with costs and orders and that kind of thing.

I have been doing a lot of paperwork. It's always a balancing exercise but I never wanted to be in court every day because I like to have time to prepare things properly.

NB: *What parts of your practice do you find most interesting and what areas might some people find less exciting?*

SD: I can imagine that an area, or part of my practice, that people might find difficult is the amount of paperwork. There is a lot of reading which can be quite dry, wading through lots of bundles or now PDF bundles, sitting at a desk all day. You are not always at court with that kind of adrenalin. Your cases can last a very, very long time. We didn't get to trial on that Danish case and it's a case I started in my first week of tenancy three years ago. There are always sub-issues, disputes, different stages of proceedings that you are going through but if you want a daily or weekly churn, you are not going to have that.

NB: *It must be quite tricky being involved in a case that goes on for so long because you have always got to kind of keep it in your mind to keep track of things and keep it at a level for so long?*

SD: It can get to a point where you feel you can almost only do that case. For example, with a case management hearing every month you have skeleton arguments to prepare and in a commercial setting, a skeleton is not something you put together overnight, especially not when there are several of you in the counsel team. If you are the most junior, you are the one that does the first draft and then it has to go through counsel before it even goes to the solicitors, before it goes to the client – potentially several times over – before it goes to the court. So these things take time. People want it finessed because they are paying a lot of money for it. That potentially is something that people might find less exciting. Not being on your feet as much. If you want to be Rumpole, if you want to do jury speeches, if you want to do lot of witness examination as a junior, it's probably not the right area.

NB: *What is the best bit for you?*

SD: In some ways it's one of the best and one of the hardest things, you are constantly learning which is something that I wanted from this job. That was really important to me as I didn't want to be bored. You never get to a point where you have done the same dispute a thousand times, you know it back to front, you know the law, you know the facts. This area is just too broad for that. For me, that means there is a lot of learning every day – whether it's a new area of law or a new type of business or a new type of share trading, whatever it is that you are trying to get your mind around. There is a real challenge there which is really hard but it keeps you going. I have met some people who became judges because they got bored of their narrow practice area and bored of seeing the same dispute over and over. In my Chambers that is not an issue.

NB: *Did Bar School prepare you for what your practice is now becoming? Quite helpful? Would that be what you are saying?*

SD: I do think it's important and helpful, and you have to have that grounding. I wanted to go into this area of the law because I wanted time to prepare my work, I didn't want to be in court every day. I wanted to be doing written work a lot of the time and that is the case. I think it would have surprised me that my work is not the set pieces of the kind you asked about, such as drafting particulars of claim or drafting a formal opinion or doing trials very regularly. It is the spaces in between in a case where you have received a witness statement and so you need to delve into that area of the law a bit more than you thought about before, or you are dealing with a procedural point. I wouldn't really have thought there were as many procedural points as there are that could possibly come up! Also, Bar School cannot prepare you for being led; firstly, because all the leaders are different and, secondly, there is just no format in Bar School for that!

NB: *Were there any subject areas maybe at university or Bar School that you were glad you took?*

SD: I did the GDL, so I did the core foundational modules and not much more really. To turn the question on its head a little bit, if I had my time again on the GDL, I would have thought a bit more about what I was learning because I was learning by rote for the GDL, using those very helpful coloured ULaw study guides. That was great, and I did learn the foundational law. But that does not really prepare you for the very steep learning curve in pupillage – being asked to think critically about the law and to do my own legal research. I never had to do that at Bar School or on the GDL really. That made pupillage harder, compared to if I had had a degree or masters or PhD in law. Legal research and thinking critically are really important.

NB: *What are the most difficult changes that you have had to get used to in making that switch from study to practice?*

SD: Despite the fact that I am mainly sitting at my desk, the unpredictable nature of practice is really hard. You might have your week planned out and then a client wants something done, or the court makes a decision, or a case that you were told about a month ago that didn't land at the time suddenly lands and you have to throw your schedule up in the air and deal with it. Things take longer than you think. Things fall out of your diary. I was somebody who planned my days quite rigidly as a student and you don't have that control at the Bar, even in a predominately Chambers-based practice.

NB: *Exactly that point you have made comes up in practice area after practice area all the time, it's that unpredictability of things.*

SD: No client ever contemplates the fact that you have other cases on. They think that they are the only case you have, and a deadline is always urgent and I find it's just a matter of strict prioritisation; 'the crocodile nearest the boat', as somebody said recently.

NB: *Thinking about your work life and how that has developed and the work-life balance: when you are not in court, are you someone who works in Chambers or at home?*

SD: The pandemic has changed things a lot, obviously. My Chambers didn't close during the pandemic. There were members who did continue to go into Chambers, but I worked from home from March 2020 until May/June this year, and then I started to go back into Chambers a few days a week and really enjoyed it. I worked five days a week in Chambers apart from court before the pandemic and have my own room in Chambers. I do not have that working space at home, so I really enjoyed going back. I am now working three days a week in Chambers and a couple days a week at home, and I have yet to work out whether it is going to stay that way or whether I will go into Chambers more. It's important to me to go into Chambers, I like my colleagues in Chambers and I make a point of going through the clerks room every day and making sure I have a good relationship with my clerks which is much harder over the phone. My clerks are all in one room and that room has a real buzz. I tell my junior team every day what's going on in my cases, and they know I'm around and there and what's going on and whether I'm stressed or whether I'm OK, and I find that to be helpful.

NB: *You talked earlier about PDFs. Are you someone who is fully electronic?*

SD: I am since the pandemic. I bought a big iPad and we all were told to get good PDF reading software. Don't bother to get it as a student because your Chambers can probably get a better deal on it. I do everything paperless now so I have a big iPad with a Bluetooth pencil so I can mark up my papers, I can highlight, and I think everybody is being forced to be much more techy. The Commercial Court issued last week said they now expect all bundles to be PDFs. The Commercial Court were used to carousels and stacks of bundles because every case has thousands of pages. It's really no surprise that we have gone paperless now, but the courts are saying that PDF bundles are now what they require so I have my iPad, my desktop in Chambers, a second screen and my laptop at home.

NB: *When you submit your electronic bundles to the court, at their end, is the court good at making sure that judges have access to it and are the judges OK with handling that type of document?*

SD: The pandemic has meant that they have had to become better at it but actually the Commercial Court did have some systems for it before. The Commercial Court is part of the High Court in which I practise most commonly. It's a specialist court for commercial disputes and it hears very high value and complex disputes generally. That kind of work has always involved lots of paper, even the smallest trial has tons of bundles. That meant that even before the pandemic some electronic systems were in place. There is a particular operating system called Magnum which the courts are all very familiar with and so most of the judges had some experience with using electronic document management systems, but it has now become standard. Since the pandemic only a few judges request hard copies.

NB: *Is your practice sociable and collegiate or is it a lot of time working at your desk? From what you have been saying, mostly where you are working is at a desk at home.*

SD: It's normally on my own at a desk regardless. Everyone in my Chambers has their own room. So I am on my own, but I am working within a team, being led, albeit normally at the end of a phone or the end of an e-mail from my leader, and won't be in constant contact with them. You have intense periods where you spend a lot of time with particular members of Chambers, otherwise I get a coffee with a member of Chambers a few times a week and I try to keep my door open. We are not a Chambers that goes to the pub that regularly or has Chambers tea every day, but I like my colleagues in Chambers and people just come by your room and chat. One of my leaders who didn't know whether I would be in or not just opened my door and came in and chatted to me for ten minutes this afternoon. I grabbed a coffee with a few juniors this morning. I have coffee with a mentor in Chambers on Thursday. Being desk-based means that probably somebody else is around and if at 11 o'clock I call round a few of my friends in Chambers and see if anyone wants to walk down to the coffee shop, probably there is somebody who will walk with me.

NB: *Would you say you have typical hours of work? Are you quite regimented in separating that out or not? What works for you?*

SD: If I go into Chambers, I am in Chambers by 8 o'clock and I will work until relatively early evening, 6/7pm, something like that. I like to run home from Chambers and then I have dinner with my partner and then I normally do a few hours of work after that. I also work Sundays. I take my Saturdays off as a rule to preserve one day properly offline a week.

NB: *There isn't much travelling?*

SD: No, not really. I travel from where I live to Chambers and home again. Pre-pandemic, if you are going to the High Court that is a ten-minute walk down the road. If I was going to the County Courts, that could be anywhere. We are not regional in that sense because a lot of cases would be small banking cases, involving any client of the bank – it could be all over the country. I think the furthest I have had to go to is St Helens. I know people who have had to go to Cornwall or Wales but it's not very common and your solicitors pay your travel.

NB: *The Bar Council likes to talk about how important wellbeing is to the Bar. It wasn't always like that. In 1994 wellbeing wasn't a word advocates knew at all. You seem to have quite long work hours, but it must work for you?*

SD: It is a hard-working profession, probably because you are self-employed and so there is often no back-up to cover for you. I think well-being is very personal and different people have to find different ways to make it work for them. That might mean different things at different times. So if you are having a week where you are, for a personal reason, very stressed, if you have good clerks, or if you have a diary that allows that, you might be able to take a bit of a back seat. That is not always going to be the case. I think the Bar is hard; you have got to find a way that works for you.

For me, I know it's really important for me to cycle into Chambers and I like to run home a few times a week and I like to have dinner at home and I have to take my Saturdays off. I don't sleep as much as I want to. I think of myself as incredibly lucky because I mostly choose the rhythm of my day; there are occasionally times where I get an afternoon off and I don't have to be in work. My friends don't have that. I have more flexibility, and I also take a lot of holiday compared to my employed friends (to make up for the weekends and late evenings). I think the Bar generally has a greatly enhanced sense of wellbeing, compared to what it did even a few years ago. I think the pandemic has heightened that. A lot of people have struggled and I do think there is a greater awareness but it definitely requires resilience and stamina even at the best of times.

NB: *People that you know at the Bar, if you have friends maybe in other areas of law, do they take steps for wellbeing?*

SD: Most people try in some way. Whether or not it's working, I think we will see in 20 years' time how those steps have worked out for my generation. A lot of people do leave the Bar, and I see that in my peers, not necessarily so much in my area of law which I think it's a bit more predictable and much better remunerated.

NB: *Very open question really on diversity, whether you have any experiences or observations about diversity at the Bar. We are keen to know people's experiences of sex equality, race equality, social mobility and any other areas that might touch on the issue of diversity in general.*

SD: There are many fewer women than men in my area of the Bar but I will firmly say that I have never felt at a disadvantage with clients or members of Chambers or my clerks or anybody, or felt that I had been treated differently as a woman. I noticed that there are a really strong crop of female commercial judges coming through, and they are brilliant and show what can be done. There are also issues with racial equality at the commercial bar which I know people are also working on. It is a good job and people should apply. I was, for the last two years, in charge of mini-pupillages in Chambers and you just want to see more applications coming through from really good candidates of all ethnicities, genders, whatever it might be. Chambers also runs mentoring schemes, as do the Inns, for people from less well-represented backgrounds.

NB: *My next question is about income progression in the early years of practice in the areas that people like yourself work in.*

SD: Pupillage awards are obviously published on most sets' websites. In commercial law they are high, and then when you start taking your own work in pupillage as well as work for your supervisors, you can expect to be paid extra for those. Your hourly rate in commercial terms starts off very low and rapidly increases so there is quite a steep increase in your hourly rate in the first two, three years. Most of your work will be done on an hourly rate. You earn depending on how many hours you do. There are different cases that aren't on an hourly rate or for example on a government rate. Or County Court work means more advocacy, but they pay less well than the led cases where you are doing hours and hours of paperwork at your desk. But there is a rapid income progression from what really starts as a very healthy pupillage award. It has surprised me how much the commercial bar pays. It is a very well remunerated profession.

NB: *Do you have any thoughts about the future of the commercial bar?*

SD: The commercial bar is doing very well. The Commercial Court has more work than ever, and commercial Chambers have more work for juniors than ever. You will not struggle for work in this area of the law, and commercial disputes are not going anywhere either. Sadly, recessions are part of a lot of business disputes. There was a surge, before I was in practice, after the recession in 2007/2008, and there is likely to be another one again. I am working on a case which is to do with the liquidation of a portfolio of assets in the pandemic. I have also done a business interruption insurance dispute but those two are the first I have done which have been directly Covid-related but there will be an upswing. Arbitration is an ever-growing area as well. More and more people choose to have their disputes heard privately. Everybody I know in Chambers does a mix of court work and arbitral work. It just seems that the cases get bigger and bigger.

NB: *Thank you very much indeed, Sophia.*

9 Crime

An Interview with Tony Williams, Central Chambers, Manchester

NB: *When did you begin tenancy, Tony?*

TW: I started tenancy in April 2019, so I was first on my feet October 2018 for my second six. My practice has been 99% crime.

NB: *What's the other 1%?*

TW: Other little bits and bats. I've done a social security tribunal. I was once instructed to attend the County Court to represent a client on an application to have him committed to prison for breaching an anti-social behaviour injunction. I was instructed to attend the Civil Courts on a small claim once; this settled the day before. I have also advised a doctor in relation to regulatory matters as I used to work at the General Medical Council.

NB: *Did you always want to practise in crime?*

TW: Actually no. As a child, I wanted to be a doctor. When I started my A-levels, I chose five with the plan of dropping one and proceeding with four. I chose chemistry, biology, history, German and law. I just thought I would take law out of curiosity but within two weeks, I dropped biology because I decided I didn't want to be a doctor anymore. I just fell in love with law. That is when the great revelation came for me.

NB: *Was the revelation that it was crime that you wanted to practise in?*

TW: That probably also came during my A-levels. The way my A-level was taught included some equity and tort law, but then my tutor chose to use the second year to focus on the criminal law and police powers. So, I think that is when it was ingrained in me.

I am interested in every single area of law I look at; I think it's all fascinating. I even went to commercial law lectures at university with no

DOI: 10.4324/9781003111597-10

intention of sitting the exam just because I was interested and wanted to learn. But, when it came to crime, I think it's just the principles behind it that appeal more to me. I know it's a massive over-simplification to say that commercial law is mostly just about money changing hands but from prior experience that can be how it feels. With crime, when defending, it's standing up for the little guy against the state, when prosecuting it's standing up for the alleged victim of a crime and the people against the perpetrator. Speaking for those who cannot speak for themselves. That's what I have always stood for; that's what I have always wanted to do and that's what I am doing thankfully.

NB: *I understand that because when I was at university, in the first year we studied a module, I think it was called 'constitutional law and the individual and the state'. The professor leading that was called Keith Ewing.*

TW: He has written a book!

NB: *He has. I think he's written a few. Just before I began at university he published a book dealing with the individual and the state, it was called* Freedom under Thatcher. *It was an excellent book. Everybody bought it, of course. It influenced me, I think, in where I went with my practice.*

TW: I think public law goes hand-in-hand with crime. When defending in crime you're defending an individual against the state. When it comes to large judicial review or administrative law, you are bringing the state to court. You are bringing them to account (which meant a lot more ten years ago when I was doing my law degree than it does now). But they are two sides of the same coin, I feel.

NB: *It's mainly defence work that you do?*

TW: If you look at the total number of trials I have done, you could probably say I've done more prosecuting. Recently, this year, I have done more defending, though I've done plenty of prosecution lists in the Magistrates' Courts. I do like defending and I do enjoy having the client there as a personification of who I'm representing rather than just the state generally. I'd say that at the moment its maybe 60% prosecuting and 40% defending. That's probably just because at my level, I have been instructed in a few Crown Court cases but I have not yet done a Crown Court trial. I have applied to become a level 2 prosecutor which is when you start to get more trial work. So far I've been instructed in plenty of defence trials but either they crack (when the defendant pleads guilty to the offence in full or on a basis, or to a less serious offence) or they get adjourned. That's the unfortunate reality at the minute because of the cuts and then the subsequent impact of Covid. So, in terms of prosecuting, it's also just numbers. If you are doing a prosecution list in the Magistrates' Courts, you are preparing five or six trials a day, whereas, if you are instructed to defend, you will be instructed to do one trial in that court usually.

NB: *Can you give me some examples of the types of cases you are instructed in right now?*

TW: When I was preparing for this interview, I was due to attend a hearing in relation to a client who is accused of harassing someone and causing fear of violence and witness intimidation. I have got a burglary on-going and I've also got an attempted s.18 wounding where the defendant is alleged to have used a car as a weapon. That one's due for trial next year.

I have just finished writing a case summary on a case alleging conspiracy to supply Class A & B drugs. There are four conspirators; three of them have pleaded guilty. My client is the only one who is having a trial.

I am also being led by Ben Knight of my Chambers representing a client accused of being involved in a conspiracy to import Class A drugs. That's my first led case as well involving between 15 and 20 defendants in total.

NB: *If we think about those cases that are on-going, can you tell me about the sorts of tasks have you had to do, because advising, drafting and advocacy are the skills that Bar students learn?*

TW: Yes. I have not done as much advocacy in those ones that aren't for trial yet. I have just done a few mention hearings here and there, which would typically be shortish hearings addressing trial readiness or whether the prosecution had properly carried out their disclosure tasks.

I've drafted legal arguments which include written advocacy and drafting in one, for example I've responded to notices of intention to adduce bad character by drafting applications to exclude, and I have responded to hearsay notices. I have drafted Advices about what evidence we want to get, what the position is right now, whether we should be making certain types of application and then I have done the associated court appearances as well.

It is sometimes overlooked that you have to think a bit like a litigator as well as an advocate. You're thinking 'I want my solicitor to send this e-mail for me'. Obviously, I can't be engaging in correspondence on their behalf so if I just type this particular part of the e-mail to my solicitors in a certain way, I know they will be able to adapt it into any litigation correspondence because you know the solicitor is just too busy at the minute to get everything done.

NB: *And those cases that you are doing right now, Tony, are they typical of your practice so far?*

TW: I wouldn't necessarily say so, but it does look like my practice is developing at the moment. I have done other jobs before coming to the Bar, but at the Bar itself I'm still quite junior. I am finding myself doing more defence work than I did during my pupillage when I had about an 80/20 prosecution/defence split and I'm seeing more in the Crown Court now than I used to. That change is just down to my practice developing. It is also due to the fact that the police and CPS weren't charging low-level offences for a while, so you wouldn't see many burglaries for a good couple of years. It seems that it's only just about now that they have started remembering that offences like s.47 assault and burglary exist. Now that they have, some of the work is coming my way.

NB: *What sorts of people or organisations have largely been your clients?*

TW: When prosecuting, obviously, the main client is the Crown Prosecution Service, but when defending, particularly legal aid work, it is unfortunately mostly unemployed or very much working-class individuals. As I see it, that's just the unfortunate impact of government policy. It's the worst off in society that are more likely to be implicated in criminal cases. I have done a bit of privately-paid road traffic work and I find those clients are generally more well-off and can afford to pay for their representation, but not always.

NB: *I'm interested in what your case load has been like and how it's compared with your second six months' pupillage.*

TW: In your second six in crime, there is an impetus to get you on your feet and make sure that you're in court as much as possible, both to develop your skills and to make sure you are seen by potential instructing solicitors and opponents. I was on my feet nearly every day during my second six. Since my second six, I am still quite busy because if you're not in court you're not getting paid. As my Crown Court practice has developed, I can justify more days working on cases at home prepping, because I know that I will end up getting paid for that work later down the line. So, I would say, probably on average, I'm in court four or five days a week. Now and again, I will take a day off just to do some personal admin like accounting, but there is no point in me taking too many 'paper days' because otherwise, I won't be getting paid.

NB: *You've also begun to talk there about how much time is spent at court and at your desk.*

TW: More often than not, it is a full five days a week in court. A few weeks here and there it will be just three or four days. There are times where the work just doesn't come in and I might have a few days off in the week which I can use to catch up on other things, but most of the time I'm available and I will let my clerks know I'm available. If something comes in, they will give me a call.

There are other projects going on with Chambers as well. We run a legal advice clinic that is mainly for LGBTQ+clients. I'm involved with that – my colleagues will sometimes approach me and say here's a client who wants some free initial advice with a view to us taking their case on through certain routes. We might take it on through direct access or we might forward them on to solicitors who may instruct us. We've had employment cases and we've had prospective private prosecutions; just people who have the kind of problems that arise in that community coming to us and looking for free advice. I can help with the clinic on days when I'm not in court or in the evenings after.

NB: *What sort of courts or other tribunals do you attend, Tony, and are they always wig and gown jobs?*

TW: Mainly the Magistrates' and the Crown Court. Magistrates' obviously, no wig and gown. Crown Courts, in person, mostly wig and gown. Obviously, we live in strange times so some courts are either not doing the whole wig and gown shebang or are simply not letting people turn up. In one court I go to, the Recorder is not happy seeing people in wigs and gowns at the moment because I think he sees them as carriers of Covid. To be fair, the Crown Court is the only venue that I go to where they do wig and gowns these days. Anything in terms of social security tribunals, you don't see wigs and gowns because they are very informal. Small Claims Court, again, very informal. I also had to wear a wig and gown when I was instructed to defend a committal application in the County Court once when the client was at risk of custody.

NB: *I have been wearing black three-piece suits for 20 years, Tony, and now I've started at the university. For the first time, I wear brown shoes. I don't think I've ever worn brown shoes in my life. Also separate jacket and trousers with no waistcoat. It was really weird to begin with!*

TW: So what are you doing at the university then if you don't mind me asking?

NB: *The University of Law started with the Bar Practice Course in Manchester. They have other campuses across the country that have taught it for a long time, but they have just started in Manchester. I actually saw an advert for visiting tutors where you go along a couple of evenings or month or something. I applied for that before lockdown, a lot then happened so the interview for that was delayed and then when I eventually had the interview, I'd almost forgotten I'd applied. They said to me, did you know we have got a permanent position available? So, here I am. I am teaching criminal litigation, evidence and sentencing, and skills. I did think to myself that I might get a bit worn down by teaching the same class three times, but because the student engagement is so different each time, it is always fresh – and fun.*

TW: I suppose the good thing is seeing people taking it all in and seeing them engage in the learning process that we did a long time ago.

NB: *A very long time ago in my case! Can we turn to the parts of practice that you find the most interesting and areas that some people may find less exciting?*

TW: I enjoy the legal argument and actually conducting trials. It's nice when you get to court and you know this is definitely going to happen as a trial; there is no way this client is going to change their mind on the day and plead guilty. It's also nice when you can get to court and you know that the whole case comes down to an argument about the law as opposed to being about the facts and whether or not the court believes your client. Getting your teeth stuck into the legal research, refining your legal arguments and then thinking about how you are going to put that into the mind of the tribunal – that's probably the most fun part for me. Witness-handling is also an enjoyable and challenging part of the trial process. It is great when you make a fantastic point in cross-examination. It doesn't feel as dramatic as it does on TV, but in many ways it's better because witnesses don't necessarily realise how you've undermined their evidence until it's too late.

I suppose one of the more interesting parts of being an advocate is when you have got a challenging plea-in-mitigation where you know it's a borderline case – when it's not just a question of how long your client spends in prison, but where there is a possibility that they could avoid prison. You know that your advocacy can make a difference! Those are the times when I find the job most exciting because I know that what

I'm doing can make a difference and, touch wood, more often than not it has.

As for what people find less exciting? I think there's a perception that road traffic cases can be quite boring. Some are of the view that they just involve affluent clients demanding a particular result. If you have got a road traffic trial, that can be quite interesting because it can often come down to the law, but it's not uncommon for me to attend court and find that I have to advise a client that despite what they may have paid and what they've been advised previously, they do not have a runnable defence and they are better off pleading guilty then and there to get the best outcome.

It's not like being an MP where you are campaigning for years and eventually a law gets passed that is the result of what you have been campaigning for which might, eventually, make a difference to someone's life. It's here and now. My words can mean that this person in court today doesn't go to prison. Sometimes that's the best part of the job – not necessarily winning trials, as people may think, but making a huge difference in somebody's life by getting them the right sentence after they've pleaded or been found guilty. It's stopping somebody's life from getting completely ruined by going somewhere they don't need to go. In many ways, a plea-in-mitigation is the stage at which true advocacy skills come out.

NB: *The next question is about being led and what it involved you doing?*

TW: In one case I've got Ben Knight, the head of our Chambers' criminal team, as my leader. It's a drugs importation case. I have conducted a lot of legal research. There is an international dimension to this case as well. This has been helpful for my application to the CPS to be a level 2 prosecutor, as well. A lot of my paper days have been working on this case just sitting down and carrying out a full case analysis. I am reducing the case down so that Ben can look at the reduced version and form his views as leading counsel. It's also involved, on some occasions, taking the lead in conferences. I also sit in on mentions where Ben can't make it because of his own busy practice. I am doing a lot of the legwork at the moment and he's using his experience to make the big decisions. That's a good thing because this is quite serious stuff and I'm still learning a lot from this case and from him that I can then use in my own practice.

NB: *Interesting that you talk about case analysis because that is what the university recommend to students in every single case. In the students'* *foundation week, there is a long session simply on case analysis bringing home to students that the examination and cross-examination, for example, must be done properly, and is all well and good – but understanding the case thoroughly through careful case analysis, that is king.*

TW: Case analysis is a valuable skill and to this day, I still do it fully and properly. As soon as I get instructed in a Crown Court case, usually the day before the plea and trial preparation hearing, I will sit down and complete a full case analysis which includes a whole 'good fact, bad fact' table. Usually, I've got 60% of my closing speech in my head before I have my first conference with my client and then, as we go along, I will perfect it, and then I will commit it to paper closer to the trial. But I don't think you can have a full handle on the case and on the arguments that you want to make unless you do that full case analysis at the start. There are some people who will say that nine times out of ten you won't get time to do that. I say, make the time to do it because that's the way you are going to give the client the best advice on the first occasion.

NB: *I agree, and also you actually save time in the long run because your understanding of the case is so complete.*

TW: Absolutely. I use a template for my case analysis with every brief. If I fill that in on day one and then I go off and do something else for a few months, I can come back to the case analysis and just scroll through quickly and remind myself what the case is about.

NB: *Can I ask about the extent to which your practice is matching or differing from expectations that you had at the start?*

TW: When you are studying law at university, given the academic side of things, you think that legal principles are very interesting. You can also think that so many cases are going to come down to a niche legal point – has this person technically broken the law by their actions? In reality, most cases involve everybody understanding and agreeing what the law says and the case is really about 'did this thing happen or not?' That is one area where true advocacy comes into play in the form of witness-handling. There is probably more of an emphasis on witness-handling in criminal practice than there is in actually knowing what the law says.

Having said that, I have had a lot of cases that did come down to niche legal points. My very first Crown Court brief was a case where my client was someone who was 18, so he'd only just stopped being a youth at the time of the offence. He also suffered from poor mental health. He was charged with a public order offence and having a bladed article in a public place. The incident involved him essentially threatening his mother then getting a knife from the kitchen knife block, causing his mother and sister to run out of the property into the street. He chased them outside and waved a knife around screaming words to the effect of, 'I'm going to kill someone and then myself'. The very first thing I did (as I always do) was look at the law and at what elements the Crown has to prove and realised that my client had an obvious defence to the knife allegation – at no point did he leave the curtilage of the property so he could not be guilty because he didn't have the knife in a public place. So I got the prosecution to drop that charge at the first Plea and Trial Preparation Hearing. So that was a case that did come down to a legal point because he almost certainly would have received a custodial sentence were it not for that. Thankfully, he ended up getting a community order to get help with his mental health problems instead.

In terms of answering the question, what were my expectations when I came to the Bar? I did expect a lot more legal arguments but I'm not disappointed by the amount of legal argument that I've had. By the time I came to the Bar, it was five years after I did the Bar course, I knew the reality was this was mostly going to be about witness-handling and trials and factual disputes. I think I still struggled with the idea that you don't need to do hours and hours of legal research in every case. To begin with, I thought that if I didn't make sure I knew every single authority about a basic assault, I'd be negligent. You can't afford to do that level of legal research every night before every prosecution list when you're preparing for five different trials. Learning not to overthink it and learning to think, well look, this trial comes down to whether he hit the guy or not – just proving that a certain set of events happened or didn't happen. That's probably the biggest difference between my expectation and the reality.

NB: *I think what you are talking about there is the triumph of experience and the development of instinct in a criminal lawyer which is something that only comes with time.*

TW: Yes. I think that's it. When you come to the Bar, you expect that you're going to be doing these grand trials from day one and maybe even addressing a jury. I have not had my first Crown Court trial yet, and I know there are others who waited just as long to get their first Crown Court trial. I know there are juniors who may have prosecuted Crown Court trials during their pupillage but didn't get their first defence trial for some years into their practice. That's another thing that differed from my expectations. When experience comes into play, you will get a prosecution list at the Magistrates' Court with five, six or seven trials in it. You learn not to overthink, but you also get a feel for recognising in advance those cases where there is no way they are realistically going to end up proceeding as a trial and those cases that are definitely going to be contested.

Suppose I can tell that the complainant isn't going to turn up – I know I'm going to be asked to make an application to adduce hearsay evidence which is unlikely to succeed and then I'm going to have to offer no evidence. That enables me to focus on those cases which are almost definitely going to end up as trials. Experience gets you a feel for which cases are actually 'runners' and which ones aren't so you can better manage your prep time.

NB: *Tony, do you think that Bar School prepared you for what your practice is becoming?*

TW: I think some of the basic skills that I learned in Bar School do help, but there's a difference between passing the course and learning to be a good advocate. I think doing everything that the course expects you to do is one thing, but then learning when and how to deviate from that is where your experience and skills can come in. For example, they teach you never to ask a question to which you don't the answer and never to ask a question to which you do not *want* the answer. As you develop experience, you will learn times where you know it's safe to ask an open question in cross-examination because you know that whatever answer you get is not going to be harmful to your case.

One example in particular is a case I was prosecuting where this lad was accused of supplying Class A drugs in Piccadilly Gardens and there was some footage where you can follow his movements through the evening. He's just approaching random people and he's passing by some couples to get to others. He had drugs in his possession as a set of deals, and as he was giving his narrative he couldn't seem to give the same explanation for his actions twice.

So I cross-examined by taking him through the footage again and asking him, well look, you are approaching this second couple here, you said initially that's because you wanted to borrow a cigarette off them. Well, you could have asked this first couple here couldn't you? But you ignored them? So why have you skipped these two? He just couldn't give the same answer twice. I was basically doing a second examination-in-chief with him because I knew he would not be able to give the same explanation twice. That in itself gave the impression to the tribunal that he was clearly not telling the truth and that he was making it up as he was going along.

But that's experience; that's not what you are expected to do straight out of Bar School. I do think it does give you the very basic tools that you need to be able to do the job but there is a level of reality that comes into it that no school could teach you. That's not a criticism of the Bar course, it's just a reflection of how a criminal pupillage shapes you. You will see reality for your first six months' pupillage and then you will be sent off to do it on your own based on what you learnt throughout those six months. So, I don't think that Bar School prepared me for what my practice is becoming. Rather, it gave me the tools I needed to progress, and the rest is experience.

NB: *I completely agree with that. I see that Bar School gives you that badge of competence to begin your practice as a barrister. After that, the rest is up to you to keep on top of it, to learn from experience – start small, get bigger and keep up your Continuing Professional Development all the time.*

TW: *The Devil's Advocate*, a book by Iain Morley, was absolute gospel for me. I thought it was fantastic, particularly if you want to be a criminal lawyer. It's less about the theory of advocacy and more about the literal basic stepping-stones. He writes the book in such a way that it's easy to follow as well. I have not read it in a while but I remember every single principle in it. I read that after my Bar course. I passed my exams based on what I learned at the university, but I learned to hone my skills by what I've got through *The Devil's Advocate* and what I've learned from Ben in Chambers as well. For example, *The Devil's Advocate* taught me to write my closing speech, or 80% of it, before the case starts.

NB: *That is also something I say to my students. If you are doing a proper case analysis as you should do, many advocates will have a closing speech mapped out which you tinker with as the case goes on because evidence takes you all sorts of places. It's the best preparation. Are there any subject areas at university or Bar School that as you started out you were glad you'd taken?*

TW: Yes. University taught the 'law of evidence' module. At the time I didn't quite understand why because I had not done a mini-pupillage until after my degree but now that I am where I am, yes I'm glad I studied the law of evidence because without understanding the rules of hearsay, bad character, understanding what a *voir dire* is, then you simply cannot do this job. Obviously, I am glad I took criminal law as a subject. I did law with criminal justice as well. I did criminology and a module in criminal justice in my first year and that was all to do with police powers and how the system works.

I did advanced criminal litigation on the bar course as well. That taught you the difference between understanding what criteria have to be met before someone is guilty of a criminal offence and thinking about what evidence might be missing which you would expect to see if they really were guilty. So when someone is accused of possession with intent to supply, you might find there are drugs in the car but there is no paraphernalia; there's no scales or snap bags or anything like that to show that they are dealing it. It's literally just a bag of drugs and that could be the difference between a conviction for possession and a conviction for possession with intent to supply.

NB: *You studied evidence at university?*

TW: Yes. I did criminal litigation, evidence and sentencing in Bar School but beforehand I studied the law of evidence during my degree. I had decided quite early on I wanted to be a barrister because I wanted to be the man in court saying things rather than the one doing the litigation behind the scenes. My tutors at the time said if you want to be a barrister, this module is what you need to do because there is going to be a lot of arguing about the law of evidence and when something is admissible and when something isn't.

NB: *Interesting to hear you say that because I chose to study evidence at university as my degree for exactly that reason. My tutor was an Australian called Peter Creighton, I found him inspirational. You do often come into contact with people who inspire you in the subjects that you are interested in, and it can be a real motivating factor for where your career begins and goes.*

TW: Exactly and I'm sure in 10 or 20 years' time, we will be getting a lot of barristers saying, I heard Mr. Booth talking about it!

NB: *Ha! Well, we'll see about that. What have been the most difficult changes that you have got used to while you have been working at the Bar?*

TW: I think, for me, actually I learnt a different code of conduct to the one that junior barristers learn today. We used to have a set of rules; now you have got the core duties, conduct rules and outcomes to help you interpret them. I had to re-learn the code of conduct essentially. Broadly, the principles are exactly the same, thankfully. It's just learning how to justify it and reference it.

It's also a challenge remembering to keep on top of changes that affect my regular day-to-day practice. There was an amendment to the criminal practice direction in the Magistrates' Courts regarding adjournments just as I was starting out that I had to get to grips with, so every time I had to make an application to adjourn, I had to learn to stop referring to a case called *Picton* which is no longer good law. There are some legal advisors, even in the Magistrates' Court, who still don't know that. I'm having to get on my feet and say, I hear your learned legal advisor's just referred to the case of *Picton*, please note that is no longer good law. Please refer to this instead and I end up just e-mailing it to the court.

NB: *As well as changes in the law, what about changes in respect of being self-employed?*

TW: It was a huge change for me, really. I alluded earlier to my professional background – after the Bar course in 2012, I worked for two years as a County Court advocate so that was all civil stuff like mortgage repossession, debt recovery, small claims, personal injury stage 3 disposals and civil enforcement. Then I worked for Citizens Advice Bureau for 18 months as a debt advisor – again, mostly civil and housing but from the other side. I then worked at the General Medical Council for two years in regulatory law. I moved from being self-employed to being employed then back to being self-employed at the Bar. I had to adapt my facilities because I no longer had the support of an employer behind me when I became self-employed. I also didn't have PAYE and things like that, so I had to have my own spreadsheets to keep my finances on track. I have had to organise my time to make sure that I do my own accounting, or rather do my own spreadsheets to send to my accountant. I've had to develop all these tools not just to help me do the actual lawyering, because I've got all these templates that I use for criminal practice, but I've also had to develop these templates for my own finances and record-keeping that are kind of ancillary to the job. I've got a spreadsheet for my income, I've got a spreadsheet for my expenses, I've got folders to keep all my digital receipts in. I've had to sort out my bank accounts to make sure I've got one that saves money aside for tax. That's something a lot of people don't realise when they get pupillage actually – when it comes to all the money you receive, you do need to save quite a large percentage of it for your first tax bill even though in pupillage you may not be paying Chambers' rent.

NB: *When you're not in court, do you tend to work in Chambers or at home?*

TW: I work at home. One of the ways in which my Chambers are keeping ahead of the game, as it were, is by having one small room for the clerks and a conference room for the barristers so we don't have a whole building to ourselves like some other Chambers may have. We just don't need it because we all work from home, we all work digitally.

NB: *How techy is it working in crime these days?*

TW: You need to be technologically aware not just to physically work on a laptop but also in order to understand a lot of cases that come about these days. There is an ever-increasing number of cases involving computers such as stalking, harassment, misuse of public communications/social media, malicious communications, the downloading of indecent images and many more. An understanding of the technology involved really helps you get your head around the evidence to advise your client or prepare questions to prove or disprove the way in which the technology works, which could be crucial to winning the case.

I suppose in terms of how techy I've got to be to do my job, I've been working from a 2017 HP laptop until Friday last week where I finally had enough money from my practice to get myself a Surface Book 3. Before I got this, I would be getting to court and I'd be giving clients certain advice and I would have to physically handwrite an endorsement – to confirm, for example, that I have given you this advice, you don't want to take it, you want to do this instead. Sign that to confirm that is your decision. That takes a good ten minutes – often that is time you just don't have! Now I've got a Surface, I can give them the little platinum pen and I can go 'right, I've typed out an endorsement for you, 30 seconds, sign there, done'. So that's one side where technology makes things easier.

In terms of whether or not it's essential, if you intend to prosecute I think it is. You need to be able to play footage at court. In court we use electronic evidence software such as Egress and Evidence.com. We need to be able to play body-worn footage, we need to be able to play CCTV. We need to be able to use a system called Clickshare so that we can project evidence onto the big screens in court for the judge and jury. We need to be familiar with the Crown Court's digital case system and the Common Platform. I think there was a time where the profession was dominated by the more archaic barrister who didn't need technology; whereas now, I think, if you're not able to keep up with the times then you will struggle as a barrister.

NB: *Very interesting because one thing I tell my students is that if they are technically able then as very brand-new barristers sometimes they will have the edge over more senior practitioners and will be more attractive to solicitors.*

TW: I think so, yes. If everybody else is just randomly clicking things hoping it will work and you're the one in court who knows how to talk people through their technical issues, you will be noticed. It can help from an advocacy point of view as well because if you have got an opponent who's struggling with the tech and you help them out, it gives you the 'honest guide' edge before the tribunal.

My pupil supervisor Ben has taught me quite a lot about the 'honest guide' approach to advocacy, impressing upon the tribunal that you're not just there to win or to pull the wool over anyone's eyes, but to be an honest guide to the court, helping them come to the correct decision. Maintaining that makes it easier to persuade a tribunal to your way of thinking. If you are able to help the court and your opponent with the technology at least, that helps to build your reputation as someone who is helpful to the court.

NB: *How would you describe the extent to which your job is less paper-based and more digital – or are you still heavily dependent on ring binders and couriers?*

TW: I was trained by a very tech-minded barrister to work paperlessly. When I turn up to court, I work almost exclusively from my laptop. It is handy to bring papers with you to court if you can, but on top of giving you a bad back from carrying it all, it's just going to go in the shredder at the end of the day anyway so I try to avoid it.

The only times I would use paper are when I'm writing endorsements, which I now no longer need to do because of my new laptop, and when I am prosecuting and the prosecution give me a pack of papers at court full of witness statements to give to the witnesses to read from and refresh their memories. It can be handy if you turn up with paper statements as a defence barrister so that you can give witnesses a copy of their statement when you want to cross-examine them on it but, more often than not, there will be a paper copy somewhere in the room or the court can get one. I have learned to work without paper.

I got a Surface because I wanted to be even more paper-less than I was. You don't need to carry *Archbold* and other heavy books. I have got a digital copy of *Blackstone's Criminal Practice* that I can search through. There was a time where you would need a wheely bag full of your civil procedure rules. I haven't used a wheely bag once since being on my feet.

NB: *I remember hauling round for many years a wheely bag full of lever arch folders and a big heavy copy of* Archbold *and the supplement and the second supplement and then the third supplement. I was glad to say goodbye to all that weightlifting.*

TW: When I was a County Court advocate I was carrying both volumes of the *White Book* around and at least 60 pages for each possession claim and I did six or seven of those per day. So, I'm glad to get shut of all that weight, too!

NB: *Would you describe practising in crime to be sociable and collegiate or is there a lot of time spent working alone at a desk?*

TW: There will be some weeks where I am in local courts, when I see lots of familiar faces and can have a nice chat to my fellow juniors and other people in my Chambers. There will be weeks where I'm in far-flung courts and I don't see any familiar faces with no real opportunity to develop a rapport with anyone that's there. When I go home, I am working on my own at a desk rather than in Chambers with five or six other people.

My Chambers is very sociable and I have developed friendships with a lot of my colleagues. We do hang out socially when we can. We will go out on a Friday night and have a drink together and share war stories. That can be quite a good bonding experience for people who do this job, you do need that. You have got to be independent but that can get quite lonely for some people. So make the most of socialising with your Chambers when you can, that is the lesson there.

NB: *What would you say are your typical hours of work?*

TW: Every day is different and every week is different. Some weeks I might do three hours a day involving travelling to court, doing a quick plea-in-mitigation, then travelling back. Some weeks I will be doing 18 hours a day just because I've got so many deadlines coinciding at once. Last week was quite difficult because I had to draft a defence statement on one case, I had an Advice due on another case and I was getting instructed on last minute hearings, having to try and manage everything at once. In addition, things do come up on the day that you don't expect so you can't always say, right, well, I'm going to divvy out my time. There will be days where you don't sleep or you don't get much sleep, but there are days where you might get a bit of a lie and might even be able to go straight back to bed for a 'power-nap' after the hearing before getting back to work if you have the luxury of time (which is rare!), so it's variable. Typically I will be doing at least eight hours a day if it's just a paper day, usually more if I am in court that day.

NB: *You mentioned there is a lot of travelling?*

TW: Yes. I'm currently based in Manchester. When I prosecute I tend to do so in Greater Manchester but I have travelled to Liverpool. In my very first week of pupillage, I was sent from Manchester to Wolverhampton, Llandudno and Caernarfon. To be fair, I think that's because my clerks thought they were doing me a favour because I grew up on Anglesey and they thought, oh well, we are just sending him home – whereas it was a little bit more of a trek than that! I recently went to Telford for a road traffic job. I have been as far north as Windermere and Scarborough. I have been as far south as Gloucester. That Gloucester case was actually a Crown Court case which was being privately prosecuted and I was defending. There were a lot of ineffective hearings because the prosecution just failed to take certain steps in advance of each hearing. So I had to go all the way down to Gloucester on a three-hour train, got all my work done in advance just to be told on arrival, we are not ready! Resulting effectively in a wasted journey.

NB: *How much of your work is Manchester-based, would you say, as a proportion?*

TW: I would say 60% to 70% in fairness, it's just that it tends to come in dribs and drabs. I will be two weeks Manchester, then I will have a whole week where I am somewhere different every day that isn't Manchester, then I will have another week in Manchester.

NB: *Before you started the job, what were your expectations about travel?*

TW: I knew I would be travelling a lot, but I also thought I would be getting paid for it, I suppose. It was getting frustrating with my old laptop because the battery kept running out after half an hour, so I couldn't work on the way to wherever I was going. Part of the reason I wanted to be a barrister was because I knew there would be travelling. I have done 9 to 5 in an office, it didn't really suit me sitting at the same desk every day. On the one hand, yes, it can be quite lonely because you are not working with the same colleagues all the time; on the other hand, you do get the variety of different courts, different faces, different clients. So my expectations were that I would be travelling a lot; that's what I signed up for.

NB: *That is what attracted me about the job as well. I know a few people who wouldn't like the job because they don't like the unpredictability of it.*

TW: I wanted variety, I wanted to do different things every day, I didn't want to get bored sitting at the same desk all the time. No disrespect to those who do, it just doesn't suit me.

NB: *Next question is about wellbeing. I wondered how you found the work-life balance in what you're doing and whether your experience is* *the same as contemporaries who may or may not be in the same area of law?*

TW: I think this is something that the Bar is still struggling with to be honest. There are still people who think that it is a tagline they can put into a Twitter post now and again and not really focus on how to actually bring wellbeing to the Bar. There is so much focus on this idea of needing a work-life balance but then you are expected to do things overnight without sleeping properly and then be expected to turn up for a trial the next day. I think the unpredictable nature of the work is one thing that causes us to struggle with that.

The amount of work that can be involved in a very short time is an issue. If I have got a week full of prosecution lists for example, it will be 18-hour days because I will have to prepare the trials the night before, get up, go to court, deal with the cases (which may or may not end up as fully-contested trials or legal arguments), then afterwards write all my attendance notes for those and prepare for the next day and so on. If I have multiple prosecution lists in a week, I will not sleep much that week. But doing all of that for very little pay is the bit that you can struggle with. Most people would think, if I work this hard, at least I can get a holiday in due course. If the holiday never materialises because of work or lack of pay, then there is a problem.

The other thing that can impact on wellbeing is the nature of the work itself. In criminal law, you will see some messed-up things and you will deal with some messed-up people and there is no support for that in the same way as there might be in other lines of work. I know that there are certain types of police officer who are assigned to a certain type of case during a rotation, then after that rotation, they are done. They never have to do it again and they might even be offered counselling. There is nothing like that at the Bar. The nature of the things that we are expected to deal with just isn't addressed by the bodies or the powers that be who want to focus on wellbeing so much. If we are serious about wellbeing, more needs to be done than just go 'oh there's a seminar once every six months about how to look after yourself'. I think there is more work to be done personally, especially in crime given the way that criminal barristers are treated at the moment.

NB: *In terms of pay?*

TW: It's not just a wellbeing issue – the proposed extended operating hours scheme is arguably discriminatory to some members of the Bar, particularly those who are parents or those with family commitments, as a lot of high-profile commentators on Twitter have recently pointed out.

But even without extended operating hours, self-care is difficult. On the one hand, people are saying look after yourselves; on the other hand, while I'm prosecuting, there is no such thing as a lunch break for me. There is this idea that you will adjourn at 1pm, you will come back at 2pm and everything that needs to be done by 2pm will be done come hell or high water.

NB: *And the things that must be done by 2pm never seem to include the advocate's lunch. Yes, I know exactly what you mean.*

TW: They will insist on an hour because the clerks and the ushers need to eat – of course they do, they are vital court staff. But the consideration of the advocates is just not brought into it. The amount of times cases are listed with no consideration for our availability is shocking. We will say that day doesn't suit me I'm afraid, can we put it on another day? The court just says, well, tough, get somebody else to cover it. So I lose the money for that hearing having to pay someone else out of the brief fee to cover the case for me, and all because the court doesn't want to accommodate me. Things like that don't sit well, and I imagine not just with me. Wellbeing, it's a nice word but that's all it seems to be.

NB: *Can I ask about diversity. Is there is anything you would like to tell us about your experiences of sex equality, race equality, social mobility, and any other thing that you think touches on that very broad topic of diversity at the Bar.*

TW: As a cis-gendered, heterosexual white male, I don't think I have been a massive victim of any issues in that respect. I come from a fairly working-class background. Both of my parents were service workers, I was the first to go to university and I will admit, I had something of a chip on my shoulder when I first came to the Bar because it had taken me a while to get pupillage to begin with and, to an extent, I felt that had something to do with my background.

Having said that, I can't say I have experienced any direct discrimination along those lines. That's not to say I'm not aware of others experiencing such issues, and from their experiences it's clear the Bar does still have some way to go.

In terms of diversity in our jobs generally, I have seen issues with the way certain demographics are treated particularly in the Magistrates' Courts as well. There can be differences in the way that certain defendants are treated compared with others. I don't think it's something that I have massively experienced other than indirectly on the class side of things.

NB: *Interesting about the LBGTQ+clinic that Chambers operates, that's a really good innovation.*

TW: We have got that clinic going on and as I say I come from a very progressive set of Chambers. We are one of the few Chambers that had a presence at Pride the two years that we went. We do a lot with the LGBTQ+community. I very much consider myself an ally of the community. Hate crime I've seen a bit of in the work, and it's mostly been racialised rather than homophobic. I have advised people about problems they have faced from being a member of the LGBTQ+community but in terms of issues like that at the Bar, I can't say I have seen it personally. I definitely know it exists because of my dealings with those who suffer it, and I would like to think that if I witnessed it myself I would call it out then and there.

NB: *Is there anything that you would like to say about that topic of income progression in the early years in crime?*

TW: I hate to be all doom and gloom about it... We are trying to inspire people to come into the job here. In terms of job satisfaction after a job well done, absolutely crime is fantastic. In terms of money, if you are the kind of person who is becoming a lawyer for the pay, then do not go into crime. Crime does not pay, even for lawyers. Certain types of Crown Court cases might be seen to make a lot of money if you are quite junior, and if you end up in a set that gets a lot of junior-end Crown Court work, then by all means, go for it. I took a pay cut to come to the Bar from being a paralegal. Only this year has it started to pay off, but with no certainty that I'm going to stay at the same level of income. I have been doing the job for two years. I would be lying if I said I hadn't struggled to begin with. There is obviously the question of aged debt – there are some clients who pay quickly but there are others who take ages to pay – if they pay at all. Taking steps against those who don't pay is difficult because you don't want to put people off instructing you on more profitable work they may bring in the future. Prosecution lists pay well and pay quickly but it does show there is a disparity when you are not getting paid the same for defence work. You can make a living, but you won't be getting a mortgage in the first few years at least and if you want a pension, well, again, don't come to the criminal bar.

NB: *What thoughts do you have about the future of the Bar in crime?*

TW: Again, I hate to be negative but we have had the prime minister publicly claiming it's the fault of lawyers that the criminal justice system is not working as it should.

NB: *Yes. He said the criminal justice system is 'hamstrung by lawyers'.*

TW: Absolutely. The story is that we are the cause of the system being held up – even though I had a trial that was supposed to take place on 1st September 2020 and got shunted off for the simple reason that the court didn't have the facilities to have a two-person trial. That's my fault obviously! I accept full responsibility for the court system not having the funding to conduct that criminal trial in these times! Sarcasm aside, I think that at the moment things are only going to get worse before they are going to get better.

I love my job. I consider myself to have quite progressive values, so I quite like what I do from that perspective, particularly when defending because I'm standing up for my clients against potential oppression from the state. If I just went and re-trained in personal injury, I'd make a lot more money and I wouldn't get attacked by the government just for doing my job. It's only because I believe in what I stand for and the independent nature of being a barrister that I haven't already quit. I like being independent; I don't like waving a corporate flag and I like being the one who is able to stand on behalf of someone, to stand between them and the state that's trying to punish them and say, 'no, you hear what they have to say first'.

When somebody is accused of a criminal offence that they swear blind they haven't committed, they will be the first person asking for a criminal lawyer to represent them. Because I believe in what I do, I will still be the one who turns up at court and says 'yes, you may hate me, you may hate what I stand for, but I will represent you just as I will represent anyone else'. One day, maybe, more people will start to understand why we need a properly-funded criminal justice system and something will change. I feel despair, but also hope even though it's harder to find.

Postscript:

At the time of reviewing this interview, I have now finally conducted a Crown Court trial. Yes, it was stressful and my client was ultimately found guilty – but my client was still grateful for all my efforts in making sure that he received a fair trial. It was everything I hoped it would be.

Also at the time of review, we are eagerly awaiting the publication of the Criminal Legal Aid Review which will determine whether the criminal bar will receive a pay rise anytime soon, or whether we will have to take action before we see any worthwhile change…

10 Looking Back and Going Forwards

Reflections of a Modern Silk

Jaime Hamilton QC, 9 St John Street Chambers, Manchester

You might think that it is quite difficult to make the case that a profession which still dresses in a wig and gown is one that is rapidly evolving. Dressing like an Elizabethan courtier is not exactly the hallmark of progression. Throw into that mix the fact that we still have many arcane phrases and practices (like using the word 'arcane') and you would probably have a point. And yet the Bar is a profession that is capable of rapid adaptation in relation to our work. It is evolving in ways which would amaze practitioners from 50 years ago, let alone the wearers of wigs when that was a matter of fashion.

Alongside my wig, stiff wing collar, bands and robes, my work tools today are one laptop, two tablets, one notebook and a few pencils. That is it. Other than the notebook, I infrequently have paper files. In under ten years I have gone from carrying endless files, at least two legal texts and briefs wrapped in pink ribbon to having an entirely digital set up. The internet, wi-fi and portable computer technology have given me access to whole law libraries. I can now access cases that run to tens of thousands of pages through my phone.

One of the strengths of the Bar is our ability to adapt. In my nearly 30 years as a barrister, I have seen the administration of my Chambers move from everyone's court dates being kept in a massive paper diary in the middle of the clerks' room to everyone having access to our diaries electronically from anywhere in the world. The Coronavirus pandemic that began in 2019/20 saw the profession conducting hearings by video within days of the first national lockdown commencing. It may seem odd that I am seeking a pat on the back for the profession simply

DOI: 10.4324/9781003111597-11

because we have moved with the times and are keeping up with technology, but it illustrates how the Dickensian streets around the Inns of Court and the fancy dress of court wear are nods to the history of an ancient profession, not an indication that the professionals belong to a different era. As self-employed practitioners, we barristers are particularly nimble when it comes to change.

In many ways we who work in this profession reflect the law. I have prosecuted and defended in countless cases that have been charged pursuant to the Offences Against the Person Act 1861. Yes, that law dates from 1861 and remains largely unchanged in respect of the offences that are still prosecuted under it. Notwithstanding the age of that Act, the law can prove to be remarkably agile in reacting to developments in culture, technology and society. We are able to continue using laws which are over 160 years old because they build the foundations in law around which a case is built. The ingredients of the offence of Threats to Kill described by section 16 of that Act of Parliament from 1861 remain the same whether the threats in question have been made by post, over the phone or via the internet. Where the foundations in law do not exist, Parliament is able to legislate to adapt or create laws to deal with whatever the developments have been. The internet has created a whole aspect of society that means both that the conduct of individuals has evolved and that environments have been created that require regulation. Sometimes the law has struggled to meet that challenge, but that just requires more legal innovation, it does not signify defeat. The barrister has to keep up with this increasing myriad of changes to substantive law. This is no mean feat, although it is made much easier by the availability of the internet and all its wonderful resources.

Law is not just about the creation of criminal offences. Its development is not just about keeping up with the pace of technology. The law reflects and forms the attitude of society at large. The study of law is the study of a living body of work. It can be in one moment an historical text, informing the student of a life and society very different to that in which we now live, and in the next moment it can be a tool for shaping the society around us. If we again use the parameters of my career – the last 30 years – we see that the law has changed from criminalising aspects of homosexual relationships to providing for equality in the form of same sex marriage. The law has changed to reflect a cultural shift from intolerance to equality.

Barristers are both lawyers and advocates. The practice of advocacy is a skill that requires adaptability. You need to change your style of questioning or the manner of your submissions depending on your tribunal – and you need to be able even to change tactic in the middle of a single question should the circumstances demand it. The most able of advocates have more than one 'setting'. It can be incredibly effective for an advocate to dominate a witness, but in the wrong circumstances it can be counterproductive. In other circumstances it can be unfair. The advocate with the greatest skill is able to match their questioning style to the needs of the witness and to the purpose of the examination.

The nature of advocacy has changed over time. That change is at its most acute when it comes to the questioning of vulnerable witnesses in criminal trials. Both the Bar and the judiciary recognised that questioning a ten-year-old witness had to be very different to questioning a detective with 20 years' service. This led to specialist training for advocates, adaptations to the court process and the development of 'toolkits' to assist the advocate in the way they would examine witnesses with particular needs, whether that be simply because of their young age or because of issues created by neurodiversity. (Just search online for 'advocate toolkits'.) The adaptations to the court process have included the witness being remote from the courtroom, cross-examination being recorded months before the actual trial, the assistance of intermediaries in allowing advocates and the court to understand the communication needs of the witness and particular court hearings to set the rules that the examination must follow.

Whilst I still wear a horsehair wig on my head (and I support that continuing for reasons more than just tradition), the way that I work, the law that applies to my work, the procedures in the courtroom and the skills that I apply are in a constant state of development. Change is at the very heart of the role of an advocate in the justice system. If we stand still as advocates and lawyers, we get left behind. The landscape in which we work requires us to be adaptable. But have barristers themselves changed?

When I commenced pupillage there were perhaps 30 members of Chambers. There were four women and twenty-six men. Every face in Chambers was ethnically visually similar. That did not reflect badly on my Chambers in particular, it reflected poorly on the Bar as a whole. We were not some outlier, we represented the diversity of the Bar. I recall going to a meeting early on in my career about fair recruitment processes. A more senior member of the Bar asked, in all honesty, 'just what is wrong with only wanting to recruit candidates that had been to Oxbridge?', with the follow up remark 'what is the problem with having standards?' This image is still one that the Bar struggles with. White. Male. Privately educated. Posh. The image is not entirely fair but it is entirely understandable.

Where adaptability and change have always been features of the Bar, change in the complexion of the Bar was not. In 2021 we celebrated the 100th anniversary of the first women to be called to the Bar. A centuries old profession, with the Inns of Court dating back to the 14th century, had only begun to admit women to the profession after something like half a millennium. The first female regular holder of judicial office was only appointed in 1956. By 1976 there were still only ten full-time female judges. The first female Court of Appeal judge was appointed in 1988. By 1994, and with the appointment of Brenda Hale, the total number of female High Court judges stood at ten – that is not the total number still sitting in 1994, ten was the total number that there had ever been.

The Bar, and the legal profession more widely, has a lot of catching up to do. The speed at which we are catching up has certainly increased dramatically in recent times. In my own Chambers (the Chambers where we had five women out of thirty members when I started) we now have 107 members, of whom 49 are women. When I look through the list of barristers of those below 20 years' call, the ratio is 60/40 women to men. There is undoubtedly an element by which that sort of ratio will mean that the number of women who achieve high judicial office will increase, but it is not just a question of waiting for it to happen. Remember: 73 years after women were first called to the Bar, we had still only had ten female High Court judges.

What the Bar needs to avoid is resting on its laurels. The Bar needs to continue to change and adapt to ensure retention of women at the Bar. We should be creative about the way that all our Chambers are run so that we create an environment where primary care givers are able to return to work. We should make sure that work is fairly distributed. Simply because the ratio of women to men now more closely reflects society, it is not a case of job done. There was a 12-year gap between the first woman High Court judge and the second woman High Court judge. Whilst trailblazers are to be celebrated and amplified, the job is not done until the trail is well trodden. The achievement of the 'first' to do something is a personal one. When we lose count of the number of women that have been in the Supreme Court, that is an achievement of us all.

It is said that the first black barrister to practise in the English courts was Christian Cole, called in 1883. He had a head start on the first woman by nearly 40 years. Look at the Supreme Court. It is white. There is no escaping that fact. Only 4% of the judiciary in the High Court or above are from a black, Asian or minority ethnic background. The figure for that demographic in the general population is 14%.

It is my view that it is the responsibility of every practitioner to work towards the profession becoming more diverse. Many significant steps have been taken, but many barriers remain. The only barrier to the profession should be ability. We act on behalf of other people, often in a critical passage of their life. We should strive towards excellence and recruit in a way that identifies that excellence in a fair way.

Many Chambers now undertake anonymised recruitment processes. To try to eradicate the disadvantages that may come from being in a lower socioeconomic group, my own Chambers only look at academic achievement beyond the age of 18. We also remove the academic institutions from applications before they are marked, so I am afraid going to Oxbridge is not on our list of criteria. This is a positive way in which the Bar has progressed in recent times.

When I began, pupillages were unfunded. I spent six months living in London with no income and a hefty bank loan to live off. That equated to progress in itself, as trainee barristers used to have to pay their trainer for the privilege of being trained! Now we have funding for pupillage and minimum earning guarantees for the new barrister. This is vital to ensure that the Bar is not just accessible to people with money behind them.

The Bar is not immune to the ills that affect the rest of society. Unconscious bias remains as much of an issue for the Bar as it does for the world at large. Being alive to that difficulty is the first step. Overcoming it takes many more steps. One of the big steps to take is for everyone to accept that this is vital and not to roll their eyes at the mention of it. Unconscious bias is that element by which we see someone that reminds us of ourselves and then we gravitate towards supporting them. So I interview a comprehensive school-educated northerner who went to a Welsh university and took part in a lot of debating society competitions and I instantly think, 'he will be a good barrister' because he reminds me of myself. That excludes others and does not recognise their strengths sufficiently. That is only one component of unconscious bias, it can also include a bias against an individual due to some characteristic.

I am great believer that it is incumbent upon each of us who are fortunate enough to study and work within the legal profession to show that this is a profession available to all who possess the necessary skills. This is where a form of unconscious bias can, in fact, assist. The unconscious bias exists in the mind of the prospective barrister who does not see anyone like them in the profession. It is easy for them to think we are all white, Oxbridge educated, men. This is where visibility is key. The

Bar has changed, and although it is not enough, we need to advertise that fact.

Increasingly there is a wide range of initiatives that demonstrate to the wider community that the Bar could be for them: school visits, mock trials, online talks, they are all multiplying year upon year, and all take small steps to greater diversity. Whereas the Bar has not yet changed sufficiently to reflect the society which we serve and represent, the Bar has begun to change in the way it approaches the issue.

So what is the reader of this book with an interest in the law but no connections to the professions meant to do to further that interest? Let me begin by reassuring you – that person was me. I had no connections to the law or the professions. The way that the Bar has changed since my time is that there are far more opportunities out there now than when I was a student. Start with social media and platforms like Twitter. There is a real legal community on Twitter and lots of opportunities organised by individuals or Chambers, to gain some insight into the profession, whether that be from direct interaction with a barrister or an online seminar.

When it comes to diversity and equality of opportunity, progress has been slow. The Bar still has a lot to do in order to change. What it has begun to do is create the foundations for change. The readers of this book can hopefully build on those foundations.

Index

'activist lawyers' 68–69
advice skills 3, 14, 25–26, 32, 44, 46, 52–55, 57, 90–91, 108, 121, 132
advocacy 17, 127, 139–140; and Bar School 3, 17, 32–33, 45, 74, 107; and civil practice 43, 44; and commercial practice 24–25, 27, 29–31, 107, 115; and criminal practice 119, 122–124, 131; and employment practice 90–91; and inquests 68; and planning practice 54–55; and written advocacy 32, 45, 91, 119
arbitration 106–107, 116

Bar Council 2, 4, 38, 49, 50, 61, 62, 77, 101, 114
Bar Council Race Working Group 4
Barristers' Benevolent Association 85
Bar School 2, 4, 9, 11, 16, 25–27, 31–33, 42–43, 45–46, 49, 50, 53, 58–59, 73–74, 89–91, 97–98, 107, 111, 126–128
Bar Training Courses *see* Bar School

caring responsibilities 22, 84
chancery practice *see* commercial practice
civil litigation 3, 4, 16, 33
commercial litigation 23, 31, 33
commercial practice 23, 27, 29, 34, 38, 83
computer skills *see* digital skills
conference skills 3, 81–82; and Bar Training Courses 46, 74; and civil practice 41, 43; and clinical negligence practice 45; and commercial practice 26, 108, 109; and criminal practice 87, 124; and employment practice 90; family practice 16; and public law 55, 96, 108, 109
Coroners' Courts *see* inquests
County Courts 56, 61, 129, 131; and commercial law 27, 30, 107, 108, 114, 115; and committal to prison 117, 121; and public law 66, 70
Court of Protection practice 23, 39, 40, 42, 44, 66
Covid 1, 2, 17, 18, 21, 34–36, 48, 56, 61, 80, 84, 87, 93, 94, 109, 116, 119, 121–122, 138
CPS *see* Crown Prosecution Service
criminal litigation 3, 4, 16, 33, 122, 127, 128
criminal practice 1, 38, 48, 62, 80, 82–84, 87, 88, 102, 108, 117, 120, 123, 139, 140; and interplay with civil practice 44; and interplay with family practice 10–11
Crown Court 1, 30, 44, 89, 92, 94, 95, 118, 120, 121, 124, 125, 131, 133, 136, 137
Crown Prosecution Service (CPS) 2, 83, 84, 92, 120, 123

digital skills 35–36, 47, 60, 73, 138; and civil practice 48; and commercial practice 112–113; and criminal practice 130–131; and employment practice 90; and family practice 19; and public law practice 76
diversity 20, 37, 49–50, 62–63, 78, 86, 101, 115, 135, 140, 141, 143
drafting skills: and civil practice 3, 41, 43, 54, 57; and commercial practice 25–28, 32, 33, 35, 36, 107–108, 111; and conferences 46; and criminal practice 119; and employment practice 90–91; and family practice 12; and public law practice 72, 74, 96

electronic working *see* digital skills
employment practice 1, 88–92, 95, 102–103, 121
extended operating hours 84, 134–135

Free Representation Unit (FRU) *see* pro bono
future of the Bar 21, 38, 50, 53, 63–64, 79, 103, 115, 136

gender identity 78
General Diploma in Law (GDL) 2, 24, 40, 74, 104, 111
General Medical Council 117, 129

High Court: and commercial practice 27, 30, 107, 108, 113, 141; and diversity 141; and family practice 15; and public law practice 56
housing law practice *see* landlord and tenant

immigration practice 16, 66, 73, 76
income: in civil practice 50; in commercial practice 37, 115; in criminal practice 136; in employment practice 102–103; in family practice 20–21; in property, planning and public law practice 63; in pupillage 2, 142
inquests 39–43, 45, 55, 65, 67–68, 70–72, 78, 79

judicial review 52, 57, 59, 72, 74, 118

Kalisher Trust 85

landlord and tenant 25, 54, 55, 65, 69, 71, 89
led, as a junior 32, 45, 54, 57–59, 72, 92, 95–96, 109, 111, 113, 115, 119, 123
legal aid: and civil practice 65, 68, 71; and criminal practice 18, 38, 102, 120, 137; and cuts 1, 70, 75, 85, 119; and family practice 12, 15, 17, 20–21, 38; and inquest practice 68
local authority 10, 13, 55, 57, 89, 92, 96
lockdown *see* Covid

Magistrates' Court 105, 135; and commercial practice 30; and criminal practice 29, 83–84, 86, 87, 92, 98, 118–119, 121, 125, 128–129; and family practice 15
mini-pupillages 16, 32, 53, 62, 78, 81, 100, 104, 115, 127

personal injury 38–42, 51
planning practice 52–57, 62, 63, 88–90, 92, 95, 96
pro bono 15, 29, 52, 56, 68; and Free Representation Unit (FRU) 88
public law 1, 39, 52–79, 118

Race at the Bar: A Snapshot 4
regulatory law 88, 89, 117, 129
remote court hearings 140; and civil practice 44; and employment practice 90, 92, 93, 99, 103; and family practice 15, 18, 21; and public law practice 58, 61
remote working 20, 74–75
retention 5, 63, 79, 83, 85, 141

scholarships 6, 8–9, 82, 85, 101–102
self-employment 14, 16, 18, 70, 83, 129, 139
sex equality 37, 49, 62, 77–78, 101–102, 115, 135, 139
social mobility 5, 37, 49–50, 62, 80, 85–86, 101
solicitors 2, 9, 18, 21, 26, 29, 35–38, 54, 60, 69, 72, 82, 106, 108, 110, 114, 119–121, 130

travelling: and civil practice 44, 49; and commercial practice 36, 114; and criminal practice 132–133; and employment practice 95, 99–100; and family practice 19; and public law practice 61, 76–77

unconscious bias 50, 86, 142

wellbeing 4, 18–19, 21, 61, 75, 77, 101, 114, 133–135
work/life balance: and Bar School 3–4; and civil practice 49; and commercial practice 34, 36–37, 112; and criminal practice 133–134; and employment practice 99, 101; and family practice 14, 17–18; and public law practice 61–62, 74–75, 77

www.ingramcontent.com/pod-product-compliance
Ingram Content Group UK Ltd.
Pitfield, Milton Keynes, MK11 3LW, UK
UKHW022018180926
475701UK00005B/917
* 9 7 8 0 3 6 7 5 6 6 4 9 4 *